# Indian's Heritage of Kashi "Varanasi"

Swatantra Bahadur

Published by Swatantra Bahadur, 2023.

INDIAN'S HERITAGE OF KASHI "VARANASI"

**First edition. October 1, 2023.**

Copyright © 2023 Swatantra Bahadur.

ISBN: 979-8223437321

Written by Swatantra Bahadur.

# Disclaimer

The information presented in this book is intended for general informational purposes only and should not be relied upon as a substitute for professional advice or judgment. The author and publisher are not responsible for any action taken by readers based on the information provided in this book. Readers should seek appropriate professional advice or conduct their own research before making decisions related to the topics discussed in this book. The views expressed in this book are those of the author and do not necessarily reflect the views of the publisher.

# Contents

# Chapter 1 : Banaras- An Introduction

Banaras is a magnificent city, rising from the western bank of the River Ganges, where the river takes a broad crescent sweep toward the north. There is a little in the world to compare with the splendour of Banaras, seen from the river at dawn. The rays of the early-morning sun spread across the river and strike the high-banked face of the city. The temples and shrines, ashrams and pavilions that stretch along the river for over three miles are golden in the early morning. They rise majestic on the high riverbank and cast deep reflections into the waters of the

Ganges. Long flights of stone steps called ghats, reaching like roots into the river, bring thousands of worshippers down to the river to barhe at dawn. The riverfront reveals the sources of Kashi's ancient reputation as the sacred city of the Hindus. Along the river there are over seventy barhing ghats. Also along the river are dozens of temples with high spires, most of them dedicated to Lord Shiva, who according to tradition makes this city his permanent earthly home. Great temples like Kedareshvara sit atop their own ghats, while innumerable small shrines along the river are barely large enough for a single linga, the simple stone shaft that is the symbol of shiva. Along the temples there are ashrams, such as Anandamayi ashram, built at the top of the ghat steps. They continue a tradition of spiritual education for which Kashi has long been famous. At dawn students of all ages practice yogic exercises breath control or meditational disciplines on the steps by the river. Finally, there are the riverside cremation grounds at Harishchandra Ghat and Manikarnika ghat, recognizable by the smoke that rises from the pyres of the dead. Elsewhere, in traditional India, the cremation ground is outside of town, for it is polluted ground. Here, however, the cremation grounds are in the midst of a busy city, adjacent to the bathing ghats, and are holy ground, for death in Kashi is acclaimed by the tradition as a great blessing. Dying here, one grains liberation from the earthly round of samsara.

For over 2500 years this city has attracts pilgrims and seekers from all over india. Sages such as Mahavira and Sankara have come here to teach. Young men have come to study the Vedas with the city's great pandits. Householders have come on pilgrimage, some to bring the ashes of a deceased parent to commit to the river Ganges. Varanasi is one of the oldest living cities in the world. It occupied its high bank overlooking the Ganges in the cradle days of the Western civilization.

A multitude of Hindu deities is visible everywhere in Varanasi. Over the doorways of the temples and houses sits the plump, orange, elephant-headed Ganesha. On the walls of tea stalls and tailor shops hang gaudy polychrome icons of Lakshmi or Krishna. And on the whitewashed walls of houses and public buildings the episodes of shiva's marriage to Parvati or Rama's battle with the ten- headed Ravana, are printed afresh after the season of the rains by local folk artists. In temple some sees the Linga of shiva, or the four armed image of Vishnu, or the silver mask of the goddess Durga. Such images are crafted according to the carefully prescribed rules of iconography and iconometry.

About the history of Banaras Mark Twain, who visited around the world wrote, "Banaras is older than history, older than tradition, older even than legend and looks twice as old as all of them put together." Besides Jerusalem, Athens, Peking and Mecca, Varanasi is the only city living for last four thousand years. This can be witnessed through every tourist eyes. As Jerusalem and Athens are having western and modern touch moreover. They changed their lifestyle, traditions, behaviour and culture which, can be marked in churches. But in Kashi even thousand years back as god was worshipped, till today it is followed with the same tradition, values and even with similar dressing sense. Vedas, Upanishads in Sanskrit are still taught in Varanasi henceforth the numbers of students are increasing for it. It is also the center for learning yoga, palmistry, astrology,

Sanskrit, Hinduism and history of 36 crore gods and goddesses.

This city has given leadership of Late Lal Bahadur Sastri, Sampurnanand and Pt. Kamalapati Tripathi to the country besides internationally famed musicians like Bharat Ratna Ustad Bismillah Khan, Padamvibhushan Pt. Kishan Maharaj, Padambhushan Girija Devi, Pt. Rajan & Sajan Mishra and Sitara Devi as well as great novelist Premchand and litterateur Jai Shanker Prasad adorned the Varanasi by their great contribution to the art and literature. The Paradox of Varanasi is highlighted as it is a lively city, with something or the other happening somewhere or the other at all hours. There is also a deep sense of peace, serenity and spirituality all around.

Varanasi has fascinated visitors like Fa-Hien and Huen-Tsang also from time immemorial, who were entranced by the city. Some call it the "Spiritual Heart of India", some the ultimate guide on metaphysics, some the Holy City, some the city of Ghats and Temples and some the City of Light. Varanasi has many a synonyms reflecting the myriad hues of culture and tradition, which it embodies. But, above all these aspects it will be more worthy to say that Varanasi is the city full of light.

Apart from temples in Varanasi there are also many other places which attracts tourusts with its magnificence. Some of the examples are The Ghats -The Ghats of Varanasi are the most beautiful and ornamental in the country. Total of 52 Ghats along Ganga embody the life and identity of Varanasi. Stretching from the southbnern Assi Ghat to the northern Adi Keshava Ghat, close to the Malviya Bridge are lined with temples and shrines. Important ones are Dasashwamedh, Harishchandra, Manikarnika, Panchganga and Assi Ghat.

Dasashwamedh is the most important and is one of the 5 holy bathing ghats and was constructed by Peshwa Balaji Baji Rao. On Dev Deepawali all the Ghats are illuminated with earthen lamps and stairs of the Ghats shine with the golden light as well as the view of Ganga Arti have now become major attraction for tourist. Varanasi Ghats reverberate with the endless cycle of Hindu religious practice - from daily rituals to profound rites of passage. Sarnath One of the most frequented Buddhist spots in India, Sarnath has wealth of religious traditions and archaeological remains, where Lord Buddha delivered his first sermon after gaining enlightenment. Sarnath attracts thousands of pilgrims, archaeologist, historians and students from India and abroad. Buddhists attraction in Sarnath are Mulgandha Kutti Vihara, Dhemmekh Stupa, Chaukhandi Stupa, Tibetan, Korean, Japanese, Thai, Buddhist temples and an Archaeological Museum, housing a precious collection of Buddhist artifacts including an Ashoka lion capital (India's national emblem) in polished sandstone. Besides a large complex of ruined monasteries having Ashoka pillar, which is the evident of his visit to Sarnath, can be seen. Banaras Hindu University -BHU, is one of the biggest universities in Asia with an area of approximately 2,000 acres, founded by Pandit Madan Mohan Malviya, is a rare centre with three institutes, fourteen faculties and 124 departments. The BHU owns the most prestigious Indian Institute of Technology, Institute of Medical Sciences and Institute of Agriculture Sciences. Its faculties are well known for research works. The varsity which has become a part of culture of the city is also known as Sarva Vidya ki Rajdhani. Gyanvapi Mosque -It was constructed by Aurangzeb in the 17th century over the ruins of Vishveswara temple which he destroyed. The foundation and the rear of the mosque still reveal rare specimens of the ancient temple art of India. Alamgir Mosque -Popularly known as Beni Madhav Ka Darera. It was originally a Vishnu temple, constructed by a Maratha Chieftain Beni Madhav rao Scindia in early 17th century. The temple was destroyed by emperor Aurangzeb and a mosque raised on the site. It is an odd mixture of Hindu and Mughal styles of architecture. Ramnagar Fort- Symbol of a bygone era, the Ramnagar Fort still stands proudly on the banks of the river Ganga. The magnificent fort has been the abode of Maharajas of Varanasi for over 400 years. It still retains glimpses of its past splendour. Of particular interest is its Durbar Hall, besides a museum where historic exhibits like brocade palanquins, elephant howdahs (saddles) made of silver apart from guns and ammunition are also on display. Some general truisms used to describe Banaras are "continuously inhabited for two thousand years" and "the quintessential Hindu city." A rich textual corpus in Sanskrit and various regional vernacular languages sustains such narratives, supported by a thriving religious life of pilgrimage routes and festivals in a built environment of temples, riverfront edifices, and monasteries. In Banaras, wrote Bharatendu Harishchandra, Brahmins engage in *sandhya* (ritual) and *shastrartha* (religious debate) on the riverfront, and they are as important to the city as its elite patrons.[1] Along with the towering minarets of the Dharhara mosque that Harishchandra described as "the two hands of Madhoray," Brahmins and their ritual activities were critical to the experience, image, and identity of the riverfront and the city. Harishchandra's notions about Banaras stemmed from an idealized vision in which the riverfront anchored narratives of antiquity and nostalgia.

# Chapter 2: The Names Of The Holy City

The names express the various powers and attributes of the city and reveal the dimensions of its sacred authority. All the names occur frequently in the Sanskrit mahatmyas which praise the city. Sometimes they are used to refer to progressively smaller units of the sacred city.

**Kashi: the city of light**

This name is the most ancient. It was used nearly three thousand years ago to refer to the kingdom of which this city became the capital. In time, the name came to refer to the capital city as well. It was to the outskirts of Kashi that the Buddha came to preach his first sermon in the sixth century B,C, the somewhat later Jataka tales tales of the Buddhist tradition speak of the "town of Kashi'

As for its etymology, it has been suggested that the names Kashi comes from Kasha, the name of an ancient King Divodasa of Kashi, or that, it comes from kasha, the name of the tall silver- flowering grass which grows wild along the riverbank. However, most commonly it is said to derive the Sanskrit root kash, to shine, to look brilliant or beautiful.

**Varanasi: between the varana and the asi**

Varanasi is also an ancient name, found in both the Buddhist Jataka tales and in the Hindu epic, the Mahabharata. From the

Pali version of this name-Bnaras- comes the corrupted name. According to the Purana, "The Varana and the Asi are two rivers, set there by gods. Between them is a holy land and there is none more excellent on earth" and in the Kurma Purana, we find it simply put, "Varanasi is the city between the Varana and the Asi.

## Avimukta: The Never-Forsaken

In one puranic mahatmya, shiva says, "because I never forsake it. Nor do I let it go, this great place is therefore known as Avimukta. Avimukta means "not let loose" and in this context it means the city "never Forsaken" by Lord Shiva.

## Anandavana

The Kashi Rahasya mentions that Shiva himself explains; "My lingas are everywhere there, like little sprouts arisen out of sheer bliss." Thus it is called the Forest of Bliss. The remnants of the five old forests are now preserved as the names of the neighbourhoods. The puranic sourves describe the "Forest of Bliss" as a garden paradise, sprinkled with the waters of the heavenly Ganga. Here everything exits and bestows bliss. Therefore, all those who crave for supreme bliss or mukti, and all varieties of living beings, desire to come and live here.

## Chapter 3: Origin Of The Temple City- Varanasi

The origin of Varanasi is rooted in ancient history and is surrounded by myth and legend. According to Hindu mythology and religious texts, the city is believed to be one of the oldest living cities in the world and holds immense spiritual significance. Here is an overview of the origin of Varanasi:

**Mythological Origins:**

According to Hindu mythology, Varanasi was founded by Lord Shiva, one of the principal deities in Hinduism. It is believed that Lord Shiva, along with his consort Goddess Parvati, chose Varanasi as their abode and manifested themselves in the form of a lingam (a symbol representing Lord Shiva's cosmic energy) at the city's current location. This mythological origin connects Varanasi to the divine and establishes it as a sacred city. According to Hindu scriptures and legends, the city has a divine and ancient history. Legend of Lord Shiva and Goddess Parvati: One popular mythological tale revolves around Lord Shiva and Goddess Parvati. It is believed that after their marriage, Lord Shiva and Goddess Parvati chose Varanasi as their abode. The city is considered the eternal home of Lord Shiva and is said to be the place where He resides and bestows blessings upon devotees.

Markandeya Purana: According to the Markandeya Purana, Varanasi is considered one of the holiest cities in India. It is said that the city was created by Lord Shiva himself. He is believed to have dug a well at the center of the universe and made Varanasi the focal point of all creation.

Legend of the Varuna River: Varanasi derives its name from the two rivers Varuna and Assi, which flow through the city. According to mythology, the Varuna River is said to have originated from the waters of the ancient Saraswati River. The Varuna River is associated with the divine river goddess Varuni and is considered sacred.

Historical Connection with Lord Rama: The epic Ramayana mentions Varanasi as one of the sacred cities visited by Lord Rama, the seventh incarnation of Lord Vishnu. It is believed that Lord Rama, along with his wife Sita and brother Lakshmana, stayed in Varanasi during their exile.

Connection with Lord Buddha: Varanasi also holds immense significance in Buddhism. It is considered one of the four main pilgrimage sites associated with the life of Gautama Buddha, the founder of Buddhism. Buddha delivered his first sermon, known as Dhammacakkappavattana Sutta or "Turning the Wheel of Dharma," in Sarnath near Varanasi.

These mythological origins and legends have contributed to the religious and spiritual significance of Varanasi. The city's ancient history, association with divine beings, and connections with Hinduism and Buddhism make it a revered and sacred place for devotees, pilgrims, and seekers of spiritual wisdom.

## Historical Origins:

The historical origins of Varanasi are not well-documented, but archaeological excavations in the region suggest that human settlements existed in the area as early as the 11th century BCE. It is likely that the city grew gradually over time, evolving from a small settlement into a significant urban centre. The historical origins of Varanasi, also known as Banaras or Kashi, can be traced back thousands of years. The city has a rich and complex history that has evolved over centuries. Here are some key aspects of the historical origin of Varanasi:

Ancient Civilization: Varanasi is one of the oldest continuously inhabited cities in the world, with evidence of human settlements dating back to the 11th century BCE. The region around Varanasi has been a centre of civilization and cultural activities since ancient times.

Vedic Era: Varanasi finds mention in the ancient Hindu scriptures, including the Rigveda and Atharvaveda, which suggests its existence during the Vedic period (1500-500 BCE). It was an important centre of learning and knowledge, attracting scholars, philosophers, and sages.

Kingdoms and Empires: Varanasi has witnessed the rise and fall of several kingdoms and empires throughout history. It was part of the Kuru Kingdom during the Mahabharata era and later came under the control of the Maurya Empire (322-185 BCE),

Page |

led by Emperor Ashoka. The Gupta Empire (320-550 CE) also exerted its influence over



the region.

Cultural and Religious Centre: Varanasi has been a significant hub for cultural and religious activities throughout history. It became a center for the development and dissemination of Hindu philosophy, art, music, and dance. The city has been a magnet for saints, scholars, poets, and artists from various traditions.

Islamic Rule: With the arrival of Muslim rulers, Varanasi came under the influence of the Delhi Sultanate (1206-1526) and later the Mughal Empire (1526-1857). Despite the changes in political power, Varanasi continued to thrive as a centre of Hindu culture and spirituality.

British Era: Varanasi came under British colonial rule in the 18th century. The British established their presence in the city and made significant contributions to its infrastructure, including the construction of roads, educational institutions, and modern amenities.

Post-Independence: After India gained independence from British rule in 1947, Varanasi became part of the state of Uttar Pradesh. It has continued to grow as a cultural, educational, and religious centre, attracting pilgrims, tourists, and scholars from around the world.

Today, Varanasi stands as a symbol of ancient heritage, spirituality, and cultural vibrancy. Its historical origin, coupled with its religious and cultural significance, makes it one of the most revered and visited cities in India. Its history goes back to several millennia. Mark Twain , the famous American litterateur once wrote;

"Banaras is older than history, older than tradition, older even than legend and looks twice as old as all of them put together,,,,,,,, It has had a tumultuous history, both materially and spiritually. It started Brahminically, many ages ago, then by and by Buddha came in recent times 2500 years ago, and after that it was Buddhist during many centuries-twelve, perhaps- but the Brahmins got the upper band again, then, and have held it ever since."

**Vedic Period:**

Varanasi finds mention in the ancient Hindu scriptures called the Vedas, which were composed between 1500 BCE and 500 BCE. The city is referred to as Kashi in the Vedas, indicating its existence during the Vedic period. It is mentioned as a revered centre of learning, religious rituals, and spiritual practices.

Varanasi has been a significant cultural, religious, and intellectual center throughout history. It has attracted scholars, philosophers, poets, and artists from various parts of India and beyond. The city's association with knowledge, spirituality, and devotion has contributed to its historical importance and prominence.

While the exact origins of Varanasi may be difficult to trace, its deep-rooted religious and cultural heritage, along with its continuous habitation for thousands of years, have made it a revered city in the Hindu faith and a cherished destination for pilgrims and seekers of spiritual enlightenment.

# Chapter 4: Historical Background & Importance of Varanasi

Varanasi holds immense historical, cultural, and religious significance. The history of Varanasi spans several millennia and is intertwined with the cultural, religious, and political developments of the Indian subcontinent. From its surround position on the river Ganges, Banaras has witnessed the entire history of Indian civilization as it evolved in North India. From the ancient Aryan kingdoms and their rivalries, through the golden Mauryan and Gupta empires, to the thousand years of Muslim and then British domination, the historical currents of the times have passed through Banaras. Here the great sages have propounded their philosophies and here reformers have come with new ways of seeing. Yogis and ascetics have made their retreats and hermitages here, orthodox brahmins have articulated and elaborated their rituals, poets and saints have sung their songs. And here all the Hindu gods have emerged from the shadows into bold relief, as people have come to understand them, have seen their faces, and have created their multi-form images.

**Ancient and Vedic Era**

The earliest known settlement in the Varanasi region dates back to around the 11th century BCE. Varanasi finds mention in the Rigveda, one of the oldest sacred texts of Hinduism. It was an important centre of the Kuru and later the Vedic kingdoms.

**Rise of Buddhism: In the 6th century BCE**

Varanasi became a significant site for the propagation of Buddhism. Gautama Buddha is believed to have delivered his first sermon at Sarnath, located near Varanasi, after attaining enlightenment. Several Buddhist monasteries and structures were built in the area during this time.

**Mauryan Empire**

During the 3rd century BCE, Varanasi came under the rule of the Mauryan Empire, which was founded by Emperor Chandragupta Maurya and later expanded by Emperor Ashoka. Ashoka visited Varanasi and is said to have made significant contributions to the city's religious and architectural landscape.

**Gupta and Post-Gupta Period**

Varanasi flourished during the Gupta Empire (4th-6th century CE) and subsequent dynasties. It became a centre of learning, arts, and culture. The famous Chinese traveller, Xuanzang, visited Varanasi during this period and left detailed accounts of the city's grandeur.

**Muslim Rule: In the 12th century**

Varanasi came under the rule of the Delhi Sultanate, followed by the Mughal Empire. Muslim rulers, including Qutb-ud-din Aibak, Sikander Lodi, and Aurangzeb, had varying degrees of influence on the city. Some mosques and Islamic structures were built during this time.

**Maratha and British Period**

In the 18th century, Varanasi came under the control of the Maratha Empire. However, the city witnessed power struggles among various regional rulers. In 1911, Varanasi became a part of British India, and it remained under British colonial rule until India's independence in 1947.

**Post-Independence**

After India gained independence, Varanasi became a part of the state of Uttar Pradesh. It continued to grow as a centre of religion, education, and culture. The establishment of Banaras Hindu University in 1916 further enhanced the city's academic and intellectual significance.

**Historical Importance Of Varanasi**

Throughout its history, Varanasi has experienced multiple cycles of destruction and rebuilding due to invasions, conflicts, and natural calamities. However, it has always managed to revive and preserve its cultural and spiritual essence, making it a city of immense historical and religious importance in India and the world. The cultural significance of Banaras lies in its ability to preserve and nurture traditional arts, music, literature, and spirituality. The city continues to be a source of inspiration for artists, scholars, and seekers of cultural and spiritual enrichment from all around the world.

**Here are some key points highlighting the historical importance of Varanasi:**

- **Ancient City:** Varanasi is one of the oldest continuously inhabited cities in the world, with a history spanning over 3,000 years. It is considered a sacred place in Hinduism, Buddhism, and Jainism.

- **Spiritual Centre:** Varanasi is regarded as the spiritual capital of India. It is a major pilgrimage site for Hindus, who believe that bathing in the Ganges River and performing religious rituals in Varanasi can lead to salvation and liberation from the cycle of birth and death.

• **Cultural Heritage:** Varanasi has been a centre of learning, art, and culture for centuries. It is renowned for its traditional music, dance, literature, and handicrafts. The city has nurtured numerous scholars, poets, musicians, and artists who have contributed significantly to the cultural heritage of India.

• **Religious Significance:** Varanasi is home to numerous temples, including the Kashi Vishwanath Temple, dedicated to Lord Shiva, which is one of the most sacred temples in Hinduism. The city also has important religious sites like Sarnath, where Lord Buddha delivered his first sermon after attaining enlightenment.

• **Intellectual Hub:** Varanasi has been a hub of intellectual and philosophical pursuits. The renowned ancient seat of learning, Banaras Hindu University, was established in Varanasi in 1916 and continues to be one of India's premier educational institutions.

• **Architectural Splendour:** The city boasts a rich architectural heritage with numerous historic buildings, ghats (steps leading to the river), and palaces. The architecture of Varanasi reflects a blend of Hindu, Islamic, and Mughal styles, showcasing the diverse influences that shaped the city over the centuries.

● **Trade and Commerce:** Varanasi has been an important center of trade and commerce since ancient times. It has been a hub for silk weaving, particularly famous for its Banarasi silk sarees, which are highly prized for their intricate designs and craftsmanship.

● **Traditional Arts and Crafts:** Banaras is renowned for its rich tradition of arts and crafts. The city is famous for its exquisite silk weaving, particularly the Banarasi silk sarees. These sarees are known for their intricate designs, fine craftsmanship, and use of gold and silver threads. The weaving tradition of Varanasi has been passed down through generations, and the city continues to be a hub of textile craftsmanship.

● **Music and Dance:** Varanasi has a long-standing association with classical music and dance forms. It is considered one of the major centers for Hindustani classical music, with numerous renowned musicians and music gharanas (schools) originating from the city. The famous music festival, Sankat Mochan Sangeet Samaroh, attracts musicians from all over India. Banaras is also known for its contribution to classical dance forms, especially Kathak.

• **Literary Heritage:** Vanarasi has been a thriving center of literary activities, attracting scholars, poets, and writers for centuries. The city has produced notable literary figures, including Kabir, Tulsidas, and Munshi Premchand. The tradition of organizing poetry gatherings and literary festivals, known as "kavi sammelans," continues to thrive in Banaras.

• **Pilgrimage and Spirituality:** Varanasi is considered one of the holiest cities in India and a significant pilgrimage site for Hindus. The city's spiritual aura has attracted saints, philosophers, and seekers of knowledge for centuries. The presence of numerous temples, ghats (steps leading to the river), and ashrams adds to its religious and spiritual importance.

• **Ghats and Rituals:** The ghats of Varanasi along the banks of the Ganges River are not only religiously significant but also serve as cultural and social spaces. These ghats witness various rituals, including daily prayers, religious ceremonies, and the famous Ganga Aarti (a ritual of worshiping the river with lamps) performed at Dashashwamedh Ghat. The ghats also play host to cultural events, music concerts, and traditional ceremonies.

- **Educational Institutions:** Varanasi has a long history of being a center of learning. The establishment of Banaras Hindu University in 1916 has contributed significantly to the educational and intellectual landscape of the city. The university attracts students from across India and abroad, offering courses in various disciplines, including arts, sciences, and humanities.

- **Cultural Festivals and Celebrations:** Varanasi hosts numerous cultural festivals and celebrations throughout the year. The most notable among them is the world-famous festival of Diwali (Festival of Lights), which is celebrated with grandeur and enthusiasm. Other festivals like Holi, Navratri, and Shivratri are also celebrated with great fervor, showcasing the vibrant cultural heritage of the city.

## Ghats Of Ganga

Ghats are the main attraction of the city. They are basically riverfront steps that lead to the holy river. There are 88 ghats in Varanasi. They are used for holy bathing and religious ceremonies. Some ghats are turned into public places, used for tourist activities like boating. There are two important landmarks called Manikarnika and Harishchandra ghat which are used to cremate dead bodies. On average 80 bodies are burned per day and fire goes on and on. The ashes and remains are collected and dispersed into the Ganga. Therefore, for obvious reasons, air and water pollution in Varanasi has become urgent environmental issue.

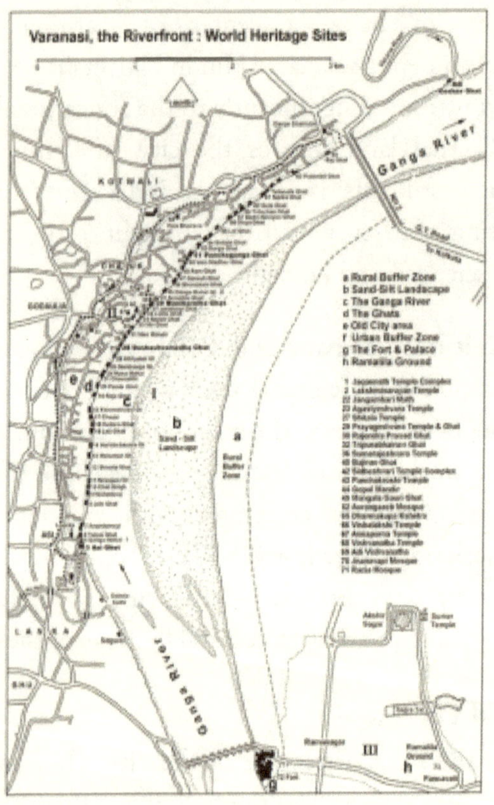


The most important attraction of Varanasi- Ganga aarti can be witnessed on the Dashahwamedh Ghat daily at dusk. It is considered as the most spectacular ghat filled with tourists, monks, men, women and children celebrating the water. It symbolizes that Varanasi is not only about cremation and death, it is also about celebrating the colourful journey of life.

Ganga aarti

# Chapter 6: Varanasi And The Rise Of Great Gods

Varanasi is famous for its multitude of temples and gods. The notion which came to thr fore in these centuries is thesism a religious life which focuses on God. The vedic tradition had been primarily oriented towards the jyajna, the ritual sacrifice. It had no images or temples, but focused upon the fire altar, a symbol of the entire universe, and the elaborate rites whereby the universe was periodically recreated in the fire sacrifice. The wisdom traditions of the Buddhists and upnishads sages were primarily oriented towards the interior universe and the transforming knowledge of its sources and sedtiny. Their rites were the rites of spiritual discipline, harsh ascericism and yoga. While the 'gods' were part of vedic and upnishadic world, and were the centre and anchor of that world. Not until the rise of theism did the gods take a place at the centre. Vishnu, krishna, Vasudeva,rudra-shiva, the devi, even the buddha gradually emerged in these centuries as the focal point of a new type of religiousness. Many of the ritual forms of this religiousness came from the yaksha tradition; the offering of flowers, water, incense, cloth, etc. but the deities worshipped were no longer strictly local spirits. They developed a wider and more universal appeal. And the attitude in which they were worshipped was expresses by a new term, bhakti. Bhakti means devotion, honor, love. The spirit with which these great gods were approached was not strictly the propitiatory spirit of approach to the genii loci and the tutelary deities of health and life , yielded to devotion. The rise of the deities and great gods can be followed in the textual developments from the sculptural artifacts and remains of early Puranas. And it is also evident in the sculptural artifacts and remains of the early Banaras. Many artifacts can be found in the Bharat Kala Bhavan museum on the campus of Banaras Hindu University and in the Sarnath museum from which we can trace the rise of the great gods.

The period of time under consideration here is many centuries, beginning after the first great Buddhist empire, that of the Mauryas in the fourth century B.C, and extending through the Gupta empire from the fourth to the sixth centuries A.D. those thousand years saw the emergence of theistic Hinduism and Mahayana Buddhism. In Varanasi, the first half of the millennium saw the dominance of rulers with a deposition towards Buddhism, beginning with the Mauryas, whose great king Ashoka is said to have visited Sarnath. There is a garment of one of his celebrated inscribed pillars still stands, adn its famous lion capital may be seen in the Sarnath museum. While the Shunga kings in the first and second centuries B.C. apparently supported Brahmanism and pushyamitra Shunga twice performed the Vedic ashwamedha sacrifice at Varanasi, they were followed in the first century A.D. by the Kushana kings of central Asia, who extended their rule over Varanasi. Kanishka was a patron of the Buddhist tradition and it was through the heartland of his kingdom in present-day Afghanistan that the first Buddhist monks made their way to China. Following the fall of the Kushan empire, however, the Banaras area came under the jurisdiction of kings who patronized the Hindu tradition, with its various theistic movements. The Bhara Shivas, a local dynasty, followed by the great Gupta dynasty, ushered in an age of Hindu revivalism, after centuries of Buddhist domination.

The whole sweep of this period from the imperial Maruyas to the great Guptas is rich and complex in its literature, its art, and its emerging philosophies.

**The Divine Buddha**

On entrace of the Sarnath museum one sees an enormous and magnificent image of the buddha. he stands flat-footed, braod-shouldered, andf open-faced, gathering up the folds of his thin robe with a very strong arm. The figure was produced by the artisans of Mathura, two hundered miles to the west, the the first century A.d. While it is a buddha, its sturdy strength is that of the yakshas, who were among the first deities to be imaged in stone three centuries earlier. The inscription notes that during the third regnal year of King Kanishka, this image was donated by a monk named Bala and established in Varanasi, where the buddha had turned the wheel of the dharma. According to the inscription, the donation was made in orderto benefit Bala's mother, father and teacher as well as all monks and indeed all the living creatures.

The increasingly sublims understanding of the buddha is reflected in the buddha images crafted by the artists of Sarnath during the Gupta period. The figures have an exquisite delicacy, made possible by the fine-grained sandstone of Chunar and the canons which prescribe that such figures conform to a divine prototype of physical perfection. In the most famous of these images in the Sarnath museum, the buddha sits cross-legged, his limbs in the perfect proportions prescribed by the iconometry of the day, his hands in a teaching pose, his eyes half dropping in meditation, his head backed by a beautifully iornamented circular nimbus. Below the seat on which he sits is the wheel the symbol of the dgarma he taught at Sranath, and six kneeling figures

There are many other Gupta images of the Buddha and the bodhisatvas in the Sarnath museum and in the Bharat Kala Bhavan of Banaras. They all portray a sublime Buddha, who certainly came in these centuries to be revered as a deity.

## Vishnu

Vishnu appears briefly in the ancient vedic hymns, sometimes as the helper of the great god Indra and sometimes in his own right as the 'Wide-Striding' one. He is famous for his three strides, with which he stretches through the universe, pervading the earth, the atmosphere, and the heaven. The etymology of his name conveys his ability to 'spread' or to 'extend'. It is this extensiveness that made Vishnu a god of universal dimensions, identified with india's most universal of symbols; the Sun and the Vedic world-creating Sacrifice.

Vishnu came to be seen as many avatars like Narsimha etc. So powerful was Vaushnava theism that the city's own legends preserve the memory of a time when this was the City of Vishnu, and several of Kashi's most important ancient temples were dedicated to Vishnu.

One of the most avatar of Vishnu was Krishna. In the first half of thousand- year period, Krishna emerged from being an ancient hero-god remembered by the Yadava clan to being a great god, with universal appeal to rival that of Vishnu. In the Bhagwat Gita the 'Song of the Lord', which began to take shape in the second century the hero Krishna serves as charioteer to the warrior Arjuna, and in the course of their dialogue, he reveals himself to Arjuna, and in the course of their dialogue, he reveals himself to Arjuna as the supreme god.

Puranas record an old rivalry between Krishna and Kashi, and said to go back several generations before the Mahabharata War. In these takes, Krishna is said to have beheaded the king of Kashi and burned the city down. There in no textual evidence of any more positive relation between Krishna and Kashi. In fact, Krishna is remarkably and notably absent from the Kashi mahatmyas. Yet while the brahmins may have conspired to keep Krishna out of the mahatmyas, the artisans were busy crafting his image for the temple.the visual texts tell us tht Krishna was indeed honored in Banaras.

The halls of the Bharata kala Bhavan showcases many pieces that testify to the existence of the Krishan cult in Kashi. There is first century B.C. image of Balarama, the naga deity, whose head is backed by the multiheaded hood of a cibra.

There have clearly been times when Krishna bhakti has been strong in Kashi in the Gupta period and again in the new wave of devotionalism in the fifteen and sixteenth centuries. Yet today, while Krishna is honored in family shrines in Kashi, there is but one major Krishna temple in the city; the Gopala Temple in the heart of the Chaukhamba district.

## The Great Lord- Shiva

One amazing fragment of sculpture in the Bharat Kala Bhavan shows a man balancing a linga on his head with his hand. Only the head, the lings, and the hand remain of what must have been quite a karge image. It is attributed to the third century A.D. We can only imagine that the man is going somewhere with this extraordinary load, perhaps to Varanasi to establish this emblem of Shiva in a shrine or temple.

Some clues of this piece may be found in the records of a local dynasty, the Bhara Shiva, who ruled in the vicinity of Varanasi and were the first of the Hindu revivalist empires, which included the Vakatakas and then the Guptas. As their name indicated they were Shaiva kings. Today, kashi is the city of Shiva. Perhaps this has long been so, but today this surely means something much larger then it could have meant 2500 years ago, when the name Kashishvara Shiva, 'Kashi Lord' first appeared. Then shiva was closely linked with ascetics and yogis, and his cult was the cult of tapas. During the period we are considering, however, the lord of the yogis became the 'Great Lord'- Maheshvara- and his cult became a cult of devotion.

For early evidence of Shiva's rise to supremacy, we must look back to the Vedic god Rudra-Shiva and to the celebrated 'Shatarudriya' hymn of the Shatapatha Brahmana, a hymn still chanted in Shiva temples todsay'.

In the Bharat Kala Bhavan there is one-tenth century bas- relief that tells a story of Shiva's ascendancy that is very important in

Kashi lore; the famous myth in which Shiva's lings splits open the eartg as a fiery coloumn of light. The haft is flanked by the four- faced god Brahma on the one- side and the lord Vishnu on the other, both kneeling in reverence upon teir divine lotus blossoms. The shaft with flames shooting from its sides, has been broken but one can see most of the story. Beneath Vishnu, as a boar, who is said to have searched deep in the earth for thw source and base of this marvel, to no avail, Brahma must have been duplicated at the top left as well, soaring high into the heavens on hisdivine goose to look for the top of this wondrous light

**The Great Goddess**

In one image found in the dense Chaukhamba district of central Varanasi, a ten-armed goddess, wielding all the weapons of the great male deities, surrounded by a host of female shaktis, crushed the demon underfoot. The wily demon changes form, from lion to bull to man, in an effort to escape. She is about to deliver the blow of death.

## Chapter 7: Temples Of Banaras

Kashi is home to numerous temples that hold great historical and religious significance. These temples have been integral to the cultural fabric of the city for centuries. These temples not only hold religious significance but also bear witness to the architectural styles, craftsmanship, and cultural heritage of their respective periods. They attract devotees, pilgrims, and tourists from around the world, contributing to the rich historical tapestry of Varanasi. The phrase "city of temples" is often used to describe Varanasi. Varanasi is known for its numerous temples dedicated to various Hindu deities. The city is believed to have more than 2,000 temples, ranging from small shrines to grand and ancient structures. The Kashi Vishwanath Temple, Sankat Mochan Hanuman Temple, Durga Temple, and Tulsi Manas Temple are among the famous temples in Varanasi.

**Here are some of the prominent temples in Varanasi:**

**Kashi Vishwanath Temple:**

Dedicated to Lord Shiva, the Kashi Vishwanath Temple is one of the holiest Hindu temples in India. It is located in the heart of Varanasi and holds immense religious significance. The temple complex is known for its stunning architecture and is a major pilgrimage site for devotees of Lord Shiva.

**Sankat Mochan Hanuman Temple:**

This temple is dedicated to Lord Hanuman, the monkey god and a revered deity in Hinduism. It is believed to have been established by the saint Goswami Tulsidas. The temple is known for its spiritual ambiance and attracts a large number of devotees, especially on Tuesdays and Saturdays.

**Durga Temple (Durga Kund Mandir):**

The Durga Temple is dedicated to Goddess Durga, the divine mother and a symbol of female power. It is situated near the Durga Kund (pond), and the temple's architecture reflects a blend of North Indian and South Indian styles. The temple is particularly crowded during the Navaratri festival.

**Tulsi Manas Temple:**

This temple is dedicated to Lord Rama and is situated near the Durga Temple. It is believed to be the place where the saint-poet Tulsidas composed the Ramcharitmanas, an important religious text in Hinduism. The walls of the temple are adorned with verses and scenes from the Ramayana.

**Kal Bhairav Temple:**

The Kal Bhairav Temple is dedicated to Lord Bhairav, a fierce form of Lord Shiva. It is believed to be one of the oldest temples in Varanasi and is known for its association with Tantra. The deity is adorned with a garland made of human skulls, symbolizing the transient nature of life.

**Annapurna Temple:**

This temple is dedicated to Goddess Annapurna, the goddess of nourishment and abundance. It is located near the Kashi Vishwanath Temple and is a popular place for devotees to offer prayers and seek blessings. The temple also operates a free kitchen where food is served to devotees and visitors.

**New Vishwanath Temple (Birla Temple):**

Located in the Banaras Hindu University (BHU) campus, the New Vishwanath Temple is a modern temple

Vishalakshi Temple The Vishalakshi Maa meaning wide-eyed Devi or Goddess Parvati, Lord Shiva's spouse, is honored in the Vishalakshi Temple. Vishalakshi Gauri Temple is another name for Vishalakshi Temple. It is a well-known hindu temple in Varanasi, Uttar Pradesh, India. Located near the Meer Ghat on the banks of the holy River Ganga, it is a Shakti Pitha and one of the holiest temples dedicated to Adi Shakti, the Divine Mother.

**Trideva Mandir**

This is a newly built temple, symbolizes modern style of temple architecture. The temple houses the attractive idols of Tridev Lord Brahma, Bishnu and Mahesh, besides beautiful idols of other Gods and Goddess are also established in the temple

# Chapter 7.1: Kashi Vishwanath Temple

For at least a thousand years, vishvanath has been the preeminent Shiva linga in Kashi. In Sanskrit literature, Vishvanatha is also called Vishveshvara. Both names mean the 'Lord' of all. It is appropriate that Shiva reigns in Kashi under this all-encompassing name. this particular Shiva Linga is on of the most important in all India and serves as the archetype and namesake for hundreds of temples that local worshippers proudly call 'Kashi Vishvanath'.

Despite its fame, today the temple has none of the magnificence, architectural splendour, or antiquity of India's great classical temples in Orissa or South India. It was built as recently as the late eighteenth century under the patronage of queen Ahalyabai Holkar of Indore. The history of the previous temples that housed the lings of Vishveshvara is , in a nutshell the history of Varanasi over the past thousand years; a tale of repeated destruction and desecration. Today, atop the ruins of old Vishveshvara temples, sit two different mosques, one built in the thirteenth century by Razia and one in the seventeenth century by Aurangzeg.

The present Vishvanath temple is crowded into the interior of this tightly woven city, and its architectural features are hidden from proper perspective behind the compound wall. One approach to the temple is from the Vishvanath lane 'gali' the narrow, winding, busy, shopping lane which has brought millions of pilgrims to Vishvanath throughout the centuries. Silks and brasbn swares, cosmetics and betel nut are for sale here, in addition to every kind of religious paraphernalia; lingas; oil lamps; rosaries; incense; sealed vessels of Ganga water, and sweets to offer in the temple. As one approach Vishvanath, there are flower merchants whose baskets are heaped with garlands of marigolds and jasmine. Entering through the doorway from the Vishvanath lane with thrie offerings of flowers, sweets, and Ganges water, they come into a large rectangular courtyard in the center of which stands the temple itself. They will make the rounds of some of the subsidiary shrines in the courtyard and then enter the sanctum for the darshana of Shiva Vishvanath. The lings is set into the floor of the temple in a square solid-silver recessed altar. The seat of the linga is also silver, and the shaft of the linga is a smooth black stone. Shiva is worshipped at five principal aratis during the day, from early in the morning until late at night. In the evening shringara arati, the linga is elaborately decked with flowers. At any time of day, however, worshipper will come, chanting ' Jaya Jaya, Vishvanath Shambho' or ' Om Namah Shivaya'. They drench the linga with water, cover it with flowers and bilva leaves, and bend down to touch it with their hands. They will leave with their offerings of sweets, now the consecrated 'grace' of the Lord.

Although the interior of the temple is neither very large not very elaborate, the atmosphere of worship and devotion is powerfully impressive. The hushed silence which, in other traditions, may be associated with he sanctuary is not at all a Hindu mode of reverence. To the Hindu who has come here for darshana, the sights and sounds and smells of the temple, the shouting and chanting and clanging of bells, even the jostling of the crowds, all contribute to the aura of sanctity.

In addition to the linga of Vishvanath there is an array of other subsidiary shrines in the courtyard of the temple. To the left as one enters is an image of Vishnu, who must be worshipped here along with Vishvanath. Near Vishnu is the image of Avimukta Vinayaka, the Ganesha of the old Avimukteshvara Temple. And in a shrine to the far right as one enters is the linga of Avikmukteshvara, whose antiquity and significance is great. In this courtyard there are the images of Nikumbha, Mahakala, Dandapani, and Virupaksha- all lingas bearing the names of the former yakshas who are said to have come to Kashi long ago in the entourage of Shiva.

Worshippers come to Vishvanath after bathing in the Ganges might also approach the temple from the north side, through the open area in which the Jnana Vapi, the wisdom well is located. They pass around the back of the temple through a dark exterior corridor where scores of Shiva Lingas are arrayed in an area called Shiva's court. They enter the temple through the west door. The open area near the Jnana Vapi offers some perspective on the temple itself. It has a central dome and two spires called Shikharas. The one that rises over the Vishveshvara linga was plated with gold by King Ranjit Singh of Lahore in 1839; thus this temple is called Golden temple by today's tourists.

The Kashi Vishwanath Temple, also known as the Golden Temple, is one of the most revered and significant temples in Varanasi and Hinduism as a whole. The temple is believed to have a history spanning several centuries, with its origins dating back to ancient times. It has been an important place of worship and pilgrimage for Hindus for generations, making it an integral part of India's cultural and religious heritage. The Kashi Vishwanath Temple has witnessed and endured significant historical events, including invasions, demolitions, and reconstructions. It has stood as a resilient testament to the perseverance of Hindu culture and spirituality amidst political and social transformations.

**Religious Significance**

The Kashi Vishwanath Temple is dedicated to Lord Shiva, one of the principal deities in Hinduism. It is believed to be the holiest of the 12 Jyotirlingas (lingams of light) that represent Lord Shiva across India. Devotees consider a visit to this temple and a glimpse of the sacred Jyotirlinga as a highly auspicious and spiritually uplifting experience. The Kashi

Vishwanath Temple holds immense religious significance, not just in Varanasi but throughout the Hindu faith.

**Here are the key aspects highlighting its religious importance:**

**Jyotirlinga:** The Kashi Vishwanath Temple is home to one of the twelve Jyotirlingas, which are considered the most sacred abodes of Lord Shiva. Jyotirlingas are believed to be self-manifested lingams (symbols) of divine light and energy. The presence of the Jyotirlinga in the temple makes it an important pilgrimage site for devotees of Lord Shiva.

**Spiritual Awakening:** It is believed that a visit to the Kashi Vishwanath Temple and a glimpse of the Jyotirlinga can lead to spiritual awakening and liberation from the cycle of birth and death. Devotees come from far and wide to seek the blessings of Lord Shiva and to attain spiritual enlightenment.

**Varanasi, the City of Moksha:** Varanasi itself is considered a city of moksha (liberation) in Hinduism. It is believed that those who die in Varanasi and are cremated on the banks of the holy river Ganges attain moksha. The presence of the Kashi Vishwanath Temple in Varanasi adds to the city's spiritual significance and reinforces the belief in the power of attaining liberation through devotion to Lord Shiva.

**Historical and Mythological Legends:** The temple is associated with several historical and mythological legends that hold deep religious significance. According to Hindu mythology, Lord Shiva himself established Varanasi as his abode and resided there. The city and the temple are believed to be ancient and have witnessed the rise and fall of many empires and civilizations.

**Mahashivratri:** The festival of Mahashivratri holds immense importance at the Kashi Vishwanath Temple. Devotees flock to the temple during this auspicious occasion to offer prayers, perform rituals, and seek blessings from Lord Shiva. The festival is celebrated with great devotion and enthusiasm, and it is believed that sincere worship on Mahashivratri can grant divine blessings and fulfill desires.

**Aarti and Worship:** The Kashi Vishwanath Temple conducts daily aarti (devotional ceremony) multiple times a day. The aarti rituals involve the waving of lamps, chanting of sacred mantras, and offerings to Lord Shiva. The grand Ganga Aarti performed at the Dashashwamedh Ghat in front of the temple is a major attraction for devotees and showcases the deep reverence for Lord Shiva.

The religious significance of the Kashi Vishwanath Temple lies in its association with Lord Shiva, its status as a Jyotirlinga, and its location in Varanasi, a city known for spiritual liberation.

The temple attracts millions of devotees who seek blessings, spiritual solace, and a connection with the divine.

**History:**

The temple's history can be traced back several centuries. The original structure is said to have been built around 800 CE, but it has undergone several reconstructions due to invasions and destruction. The current temple complex was constructed by the Maratha ruler, Maharani Ahilyabai Holkar, in the 18th century. The history of the Kashi Vishwanath Temple, one of the most revered Hindu temples in Varanasi, stretches back several centuries. The temple has undergone multiple constructions, destructions, and renovations throughout its history.

**Here is an overview of its historical journey:**

**Early History:** The original temple is believed to have been built during the 8th century by King Harishchandra of the Chandravanshi dynasty. However, historical records and archaeological evidence regarding the early history of the temple are limited.

**Destructions and Reconstructions:** The Kashi Vishwanath Temple faced numerous instances of destruction by foreign invaders and rulers over the centuries. The first recorded instance of destruction occurred in the 12th century when the temple was demolished by Qutb-ud-din Aibak, the founder of the Delhi Sultanate. It was reconstructed by a Hindu king, possibly in the 13th century.

**Rebuilding by Raja Man Singh:** In the 16th century, the temple was destroyed once again, this time by Mughal emperor Aurangzeb. The temple site was occupied by the Gyanvapi Mosque. However, Raja Man Singh of Amber (Jaipur) rebuilt the temple nearby during the reign of Emperor Akbar. The mosque still exists adjacent to the current temple complex.

**Maratha Influence:** In the 18th century, the Marathas, under the leadership of Rani Ahilyabai Holkar of Indore, became patrons of the temple. Rani Ahilyabai Holkar initiated the construction of the present-day temple in 1780. The temple complex was expanded and renovated during her reign, resulting in the magnificent structure that stands today.

**Recent Renovations:** In more recent times, the Kashi Vishwanath Temple has undergone several restoration and renovation projects. In the early 20th century, the temple was reconstructed using gold-plated domes and spires through the efforts of wealthy patrons and devotees. The current structure, adorned with intricate carvings and designs, is the result of these renovations.

**Ongoing Maintenance:** The temple is currently managed and maintained by the government of Uttar Pradesh and the Kashi Vishwanath Temple Trust. Regular upkeep and restoration work continue to preserve the temple's historical and architectural integrity.

Throughout its history, the Kashi Vishwanath Temple has withstood the test of time, facing destruction and rebuilding multiple times. Despite challenges, it remains an important pilgrimage site and a symbol of devotion to Lord Shiva. The temple's rich historical journey is a testament to the deep spiritual and cultural significance it holds for millions of devotees.

**Architecture:**

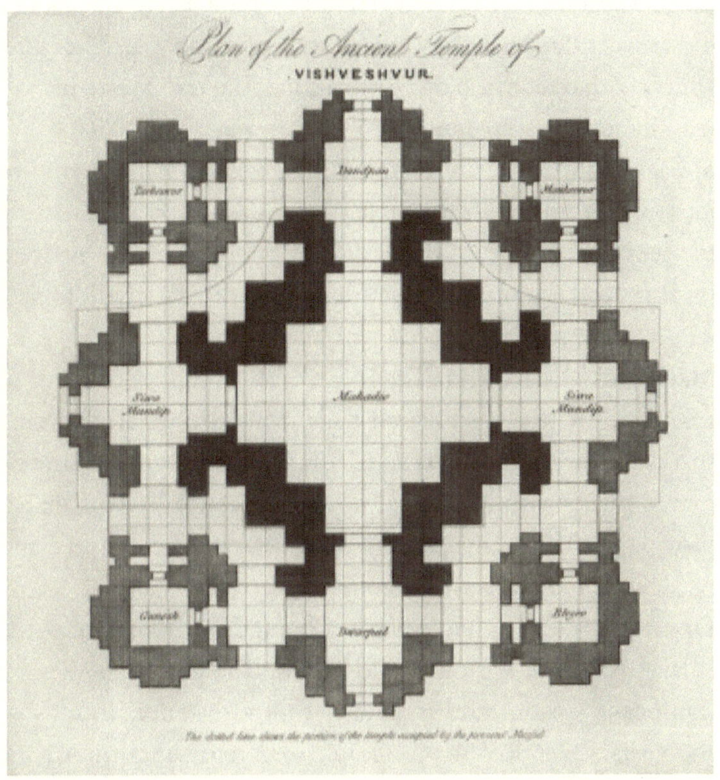

The Kashi Vishwanath Temple exhibits a blend of North Indian and Mughal architectural styles. The main temple, made of stone, features intricate carvings and a shikhara (spire) adorned with a golden kalash (dome). The temple complex also includes smaller shrines, mandapas (pillared halls), and courtyards. The architecture of the Kashi Vishwanath Temple in Varanasi is a magnificent blend of North Indian and Mughal architectural styles. The temple complex has undergone several reconstructions and renovations over the centuries.

**Here are some notable architectural features of the temple:**

**Main Structure:** The main temple is built using stone, and its structure follows the Nagara style of temple architecture, which is characteristic of North India. The temple stands tall with its soaring spires and intricately carved walls.

**Shikhara (Spire):** The temple's shikhara, or spire, is one of its most prominent features. It rises majestically, accentuating the temple's grandeur. The shikhara is adorned with intricate carvings and sculptures depicting various deities, mythological scenes, and motifs.

**Mandapa (Pillared Hall):** The temple complex consists of several mandapas, or pillared halls, which serve as gathering spaces for devotees and visitors. These halls feature elaborately carved pillars with intricate designs and motifs. The mandapas provide a sheltered space for devotees to offer prayers and participate in religious ceremonies.

**Domed Roof:** The temple has a domed roof, known as the kalash, which is typically gold-plated. The golden dome is a significant symbol and is visible from a distance. It adds to the visual splendor of the temple and represents the divine presence within.

**Carvings and Sculptures:** The walls of the Kashi Vishwanath Temple are adorned with intricate carvings and sculptures that depict various Hindu deities, mythological stories, and celestial beings. The carvings showcase a high level of craftsmanship and attention to detail, reflecting the artistic brilliance of the artisans of that era.

**Courtyards:** The temple complex encompasses spacious courtyards, providing open spaces for devotees to gather, meditate, and engage in religious activities. The courtyards are often adorned with decorative elements such as pillars, arches, and statues.

**Entrance Gates:** The temple complex features beautifully designed entrance gates that serve as the main points of entry. These gates are often adorned with decorative motifs, sculptures, and inscriptions, further enhancing the aesthetic appeal of the temple.

The architecture of the Kashi Vishwanath Temple exemplifies the rich cultural and artistic heritage of Varanasi. Its intricate carvings, grand spires, and ornate structures showcase the skill and creativity of the craftsmen who contributed to its construction over the centuries. The temple stands as a testament to the architectural brilliance of ancient India.

**Sanctum Sanctorum:** The sanctum sanctorum of the temple houses the revered Jyotirlinga of Lord Shiva. The lingam is believed to represent the infinite cosmic energy and is a focal point of devotion for millions of worshippers. Non-Hindus are not permitted to enter the innermost sanctum but can offer prayers from the outer hall.

**Rituals and Festivals:** The Kashi Vishwanath Temple is known for its daily rituals, including aarti (devotional ceremony) performed multiple times throughout the day. The Ganga Aarti, a grand worship ceremony held in the evening at the Dashashwamedh Ghat, attracts a large gathering of devotees. The temple also sees a significant influx of devotees during festivals like Mahashivratri.

**Access:** The Kashi Vishwanath Temple is located in the crowded lanes of Varanasi's old city, near the Dashashwamedh Ghat. Due to its central location, the temple can be accessed through narrow lanes that are often bustling with devotees.

## Kashi Vishvanath Temple Plan

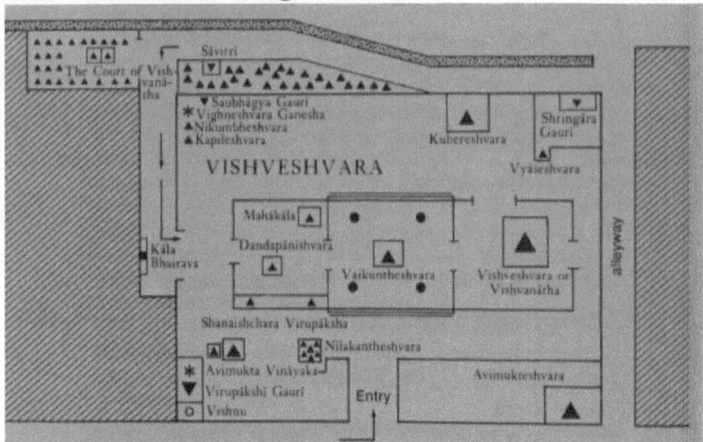


## The Wall Of Wisdom –Jnana Vapi

**JNANA VAPI PAVILION, Entry to Vishvanath Temple in the left of the great pipal tree**

The wisdom well, a deep well about ten feet in diameter, is set today in a spacious columned arcade which was built to house it in 1828. Here pilgrims come to sip the waters and take a vow of intention [Sankalp] at the outset of many a pilgrimage in and around Banaras, and here they return at the end of the pilgrimage to sip the waters again and to relax in the coll shade of the colonmade.

This is one of the Kashi's most famous wells, said to have been dug by Shiva himself in order to cool the Linga of Vishveshvara with water. This took place, 'in the beginning', when there was no water on earth. The waters that emerged here when Shiva dug the earth with his trident were the first pure waters. The water is said to be a liquid form of 'Jnana', enlightening wisdom. This well of liquid wisdom is said to have been here in Kashi long before the Ganges came to earth.

Today the well has been equipped with iron bars across the top which, according to the brahman who has Jnana Vapi in his charge, were installed to prevent the occasional suicides of liberation seekers who would plunge into the well, happy to die in Kashi. In addition, a cloth has been spread over the iron grill to prevent the coins of pilgrims from plunging into the well. Thus, one cannot see the sacred waters today, but they are drawn up daily and ladled out to worshippers who sip these before entering Vishvanath temple for darshana.

# Chapter 7.2: Sankat Mochan Hanuman Temple

The Sankat Mochan Hanuman Temple is a famous Hindu temple located in the holy city of Varanasi, Uttar Pradesh, India. It is dedicated to Lord Hanuman, the monkey god and an ardent devotee of Lord Rama. The temple is considered to be one of the holiest and most revered places of worship in Varanasi.

The Sankat Mochan Hanuman Temple holds great significance among devotees, who believe that Lord Hanuman has the power to alleviate their troubles and bring them relief from various problems and challenges. "Sankat Mochan" translates to "reliever of troubles," reflecting the temple's primary purpose. The temple has a rich history that dates back several centuries. It was established by the Hindu saint Tulsidas, who is known for his epic poem Ramcharitmanas. Tulsidas is believed to have had a vision of Lord Hanuman at the very spot where the temple stands today. Since then, the temple has been an important pilgrimage site for devotees of Lord Hanuman.

The Sankat Mochan Hanuman Temple attracts a large number of visitors and devotees throughout the year, but especially during Tuesdays and Saturdays, which are considered auspicious days for worshiping Lord Hanuman. The temple is known for its peaceful ambiance and the continuous chanting of the Hanuman Chalisa, a devotional hymn dedicated to Lord Hanuman.

Apart from its religious significance, the Sankat Mochan Hanuman Temple is involved in various philanthropic activities. It runs a charitable hospital that provides medical care to the underprivileged, as well as educational initiatives and environmental conservation efforts.

The Sankat Mochan Hanuman Temple in Varanasi has a rich and interesting history that spans several centuries. Here is a brief overview:

**Establishment by Tulsidas:**

The temple is believed to have been established by the renowned Hindu saint, poet, and philosopher Tulsidas. Tulsidas is best known for his epic poem Ramcharitmanas, which narrates the story of Lord Rama. It is said that Tulsidas had a divine vision of Lord Hanuman at the site where the temple stands today. Inspired by this experience, he decided to build a temple dedicated to Lord Hanuman at the spot.

**Devotional Significance:**

The Sankat Mochan Hanuman Temple holds immense devotional significance among devotees. It is believed that Lord Hanuman has the power to alleviate difficulties and troubles ("sankat") faced by his devotees. The temple is known as the "Sankat Mochan" temple, which translates to "the reliever of troubles." Devotees visit the temple to seek the blessings of Lord Hanuman and pray for the resolution of their problems.

**Role in Indian Independence Movement:**

The Sankat Mochan Hanuman Temple played a significant role during the Indian independence movement. It served as a meeting place and center for freedom fighters, who would gather here to plan and discuss strategies against British colonial rule. Many prominent leaders, including Pandit Madan Mohan Malaviya, used the temple as a platform to inspire and mobilize the masses for the freedom struggle.

**Philanthropic Initiatives:**

The Sankat Mochan Hanuman Temple is not only a place of worship but also actively involved in various philanthropic activities. It runs a charitable hospital that provides medical services to the underprivileged. The temple also undertakes initiatives in education, including schools and scholarships for economically disadvantaged students. Additionally, it promotes environmental conservation through tree plantation drives and awareness campaigns.

The Sankat Mochan Hanuman Temple has grown in popularity over the years, attracting a large number of devotees from all over India and beyond. It is known for its peaceful ambiance, serene surroundings, and the continuous recitation of the Hanuman Chalisa, a devotional hymn dedicated to Lord Hanuman. The temple continues to play a vital role in the spiritual, cultural, and social life of Varanasi.

# Chapter 7.3: Durga Kund Mandir

The Durga Kund Mandir holds great spiritual significance and is considered one of the important temples in Varanasi. It attracts devotees and tourists throughout the year, with a particularly vibrant atmosphere during Navratri. The temple is not only a place of worship but also an architectural marvel that showcases the artistic traditions of the region. It is dedicated to Goddess Durga, who is regarded as the divine mother and the embodiment of feminine power.

Location: The temple is situated near the Durga Kund (pond), which is believed to be the spot where the goddess Durga rested after annihilating the demon Mahishasura. It is located in the southern part of Varanasi, near the famous Tulsi Ghat.

## Architecture

\

The Durga Kund Mandir showcases a blend of North Indian and Nagara architectural styles. The temple structure features a multi-tiered shikara (tower) adorned with intricate carvings and sculptures. The sanctum sanctorum houses the idol of Goddess Durga, along with other deities such as Lord Shiva, Lord Ganesh, and Goddess Saraswati. The Durga Kund Mandir in Varanasi showcases a unique architectural style that blends elements of North Indian and Nagara architectural traditions.

**Here are some key features of the temple's architecture:**

**Shikara Style:** The Durga Kund Mandir features a prominent shikara (tower) that is characteristic of North Indian temple architecture. The shikara is a multi-tiered structure that rises above the main sanctum sanctorum (garbhagriha). The shikara of the temple is adorned with intricate carvings, sculptures, and decorative motifs.

**Ornate Facade:** The temple facade is intricately carved with delicate designs, including floral patterns, geometric shapes, and mythological figures. The carvings showcase the fine craftsmanship and attention to detail. The entrance of the temple is often adorned with sculpted pillars and ornamental arches.

**Mandapa (Pillared Hall):** The Durga Kund Mandir typically has a mandapa, a pillared hall or pavilion, which serves as a space for devotees to gather and offer prayers. The mandapa is supported by elaborately carved pillars, often featuring figures from Hindu mythology. The ceiling of the mandapa may display artistic motifs or mythological scenes.

**Garbhagriha (Sanctum Sanctorum):** The inner sanctum of the temple, known as the garbhagriha, houses the main idol or deity of Goddess Durga. The garbhagriha is considered the most sacred space in the temple and is usually a simple chamber with minimal decorations. The idol of Goddess Durga is adorned with ornaments and traditional clothing.

**Central Dome:** The temple may have a central dome above the sanctum sanctorum, adding to the architectural grandeur. The dome is often decorated with intricate carvings and motifs, creating a visually captivating element.

**Open Courtyard:** The temple complex may include an open courtyard where devotees can gather and participate in religious rituals and ceremonies. The courtyard may have smaller shrines dedicated to other deities, such as Lord Shiva, Lord Ganesh, or Goddess Saraswati.

The architecture of the Durga Kund Mandir reflects the artistic heritage and cultural traditions of the region. It combines the distinctive elements of North Indian temple architecture with its own unique style, making it a significant landmark in Varanasi. The intricate carvings, ornamental details, and structural design contribute to the temple's aesthetic appeal and spiritual ambiance.

**History And Historical Significance**

The history of the Durga Kund Mandir in Varanasi is closely associated with the legend of the goddess Durga and her victory over the demon Mahishasura. While the exact date of the temple's establishment is not well-documented, it is believed to have been built in the 18th century by Queen Narayani Devi, the wife of Raja Balwant Singh of Varanasi. The temple has a rich historical background. It is believed to have been constructed in the 18th century by Bengali Maharani (Queen) Narayani Devi, who was the wife of Raja Balwant Singh of Varanasi. Queen Narayani Devi was a devout devotee of Goddess Durga and built the temple to honor and worship the deity.

**Navratri Celebrations:** The Durga Kund Mandir is particularly famous for its grand celebration of Navratri, a nine-night festival dedicated to Goddess Durga. During this festival, the temple premises come alive with elaborate decorations, devotional music, and cultural performances. Devotees from far and wide visit the temple to seek the blessings of Goddess Durga and participate in the festivities.

**Durga Kund:** The temple is situated near the Durga Kund, a sacred pond associated with various legends and mythological stories. It is believed that taking a holy dip in the Kund (pond) and performing prayers at the temple can cleanse one's sins and bring spiritual purification.

According to popular belief and local legends, the temple is located near the spot where the goddess Durga rested after defeating the buffalo demon Mahishasura. It is said that the goddess emerged victorious after a fierce battle with Mahishasura and then rested near the pond, which is now known as the Durga Kund.

The construction of the Durga Kund Mandir by Queen Narayani Devi was a testament to her devotion to Goddess Durga. She wanted to honor the goddess and provide a place of worship for the people of Varanasi. The temple served as a focal point for the community to gather and offer their prayers to the divine mother.

Over the centuries, the temple has witnessed various renovations and additions to its structure. These renovations have been undertaken by devotees, local communities, and subsequent rulers who wanted to maintain and enhance the temple's spiritual significance. These renovations have contributed to the temple's architectural beauty and helped preserve its historical heritage.

The Durga Kund Mandir has been an important religious and cultural center in Varanasi. It has attracted devotees from far and wide, particularly during the Navratri festival, which is dedicated to the worship of Goddess Durga. The temple continues to be an essential site for devotees seeking the blessings and protection of the goddess.

Today, the Durga Kund Mandir stands as a testament to the devotion and architectural splendor associated with the worship of Goddess Durga in Varanasi. It holds deep spiritual and historical significance, drawing devotees and tourists alike to experience its religious aura and learn about its rich heritage.

# Chapter 7.4: Tulsi Manas Temple

One of Varanasi's most well-known temples, Tulsi Manas Mandir is also known as Tulsi Birla Manas Mandir. It is situated near Durgakund in Varanasi, not far from the Durga Temple. It was constructed in 1964 using white marble and has a lovely garden, which makes it look quite charming. The Banaras family built the temple, which is devoted to Lord Rama. Beautiful statues of Ram, Sita, Lakshman, and Hanuman can be found in the temple.

The Durga Temple, Sankat Mochan Temple, and New Vishwanath Temple are three other temples that are close to the Tulsi Manas Mandir. It is now the focal focus of the Kashi tourist industry. It is said that the temple was erected on the site where the revered poet Goswami Tulsidas wrote the classic Indian epic Ramcharitamanasa. Several scenes from the Ramcharitamanas can be seen on the temple wall.

**Location:**

The Tulsi Manas Temple is located in the Durgakund area of Varanasi, close to the Tulsi Ghat. The temple stands on the spot where Tulsidas, the author of the famous epic poem Ramcharitmanas, is believed to have composed this literary masterpiece.

**Architecture:**

The temple follows the Nagara architectural style, prevalent in North India. The structure is made of white marble and features intricate carvings and engravings from the Ramcharitmanas, depicting the life and exploits of Lord Rama. The walls of the temple are adorned with verses and images from the epic, providing a visual representation of Tulsidas' work.

The Tulsi Manas Temple in Varanasi features an architectural style that blends traditional and modern elements.

**Here are the key architectural aspects of the temple:**

**Structure:** The Tulsi Manas Temple is built using white marble, which gives it an elegant and pristine appearance. The temple has multiple levels and consists of a central tower with smaller spires and domes. The overall design follows the Nagara architectural style, which is characterized by its curvilinear shape and tower-like structures.

**Carvings and Engravings:** The temple is renowned for its intricate carvings and engravings that adorn the walls, pillars, and doorways. These carvings depict scenes from the Ramcharitmanas, the epic poem composed by Tulsidas. The verses from the Ramcharitmanas are inscribed on the walls, providing a visual representation of Tulsidas' work and the life of Lord Rama.

**Frescoes and Paintings:** The interiors of the temple feature vibrant frescoes and paintings that depict various episodes from the Ramayana, including Lord Rama's birth, his victories over demons, and his return to Ayodhya. These colorful artworks add a visual richness and storytelling element to the temple's ambiance.

**Temple Complex:** The Tulsi Manas Temple comprises not only the main shrine dedicated to Lord Rama but also a surrounding complex that includes other shrines and facilities. The complex often includes a meditation hall, a prayer hall, and a museum that showcases artifacts related to Lord Rama and the Ramayana.

**Gardens and Landscaping:** The temple complex is well-maintained and often features beautifully landscaped gardens and pathways. These elements contribute to the serene and peaceful environment surrounding the temple, providing a conducive atmosphere for prayer, meditation, and contemplation.

The architecture of the Tulsi Manas Temple combines the traditional aspects of temple design with artistic expressions from the Ramayana. The intricate carvings, engravings, and artwork create a visually captivating experience for visitors. The temple's architecture not only reflects the religious significance of Lord Rama but also serves as a testament to the cultural and literary heritage of Tulsidas and his epic poem, the Ramcharitmanas.

**Historical Significance:**

The Tulsi Manas Temple holds a special place in the hearts of devotees as it is believed to be the place where Tulsidas wrote the Ramcharitmanas, an important religious text in Hinduism. It is said that Tulsidas was inspired by Lord Rama himself to create this work, which became instrumental in spreading the teachings of Lord Rama to the masses.

**Devotional Significance:**

The temple is a popular pilgrimage site for devotees of Lord Rama. Visitors can recite verses from the Ramcharitmanas and offer prayers to Lord Rama and other deities. The serene ambiance and spiritual atmosphere of the temple make it an ideal place for meditation and reflection.

**Cultural Heritage:**

The Tulsi Manas Temple is not just a religious site but also a center of cultural heritage. The walls of the temple depict scenes and stories from the Ramayana, and the complex also includes a museum that showcases various artifacts and sculptures related to Lord Rama and his epic journey.

Visiting the Tulsi Manas Temple provides an opportunity to delve into the spiritual and cultural legacy of Lord Rama and Tulsidas. The temple offers devotees and visitors a chance to connect with the divine, immerse themselves in the teachings of Lord Rama, and appreciate the artistic craftsmanship of the temple's architecture.

# Chapter 7.5: Kal Bhairav Temple

The Kal Bhairav Temple is a significant Hindu temple located in Varanasi, Uttar Pradesh, India. It is dedicated to Lord Bhairav, a fierce form of Lord Shiva associated with protection and destruction. The temple is known for its association with the unique tradition of offering liquor as an offering to the deity.

**Location:** The Kal Bhairav Temple is situated in the Visheshar Ganj area of Varanasi, near the Vishalakshi Temple and the famous Vishwanath Temple (also known as the Kashi Vishwanath Temple). The temple complex has a distinctive and ancient feel, with stone structures and carvings.

**Deity:** The temple is dedicated to Lord Kal Bhairav, an embodiment of Lord Shiva in his fierce and protective form. Lord Bhairav is believed to guard the city of Varanasi and its devotees. He is often depicted with a fearsome appearance, adorned with serpents, holding a trident (trishul), and wearing a garland of skulls.

**Unique Rituals:** The Kal Bhairav Temple is known for its distinct rituals and offerings. One of the notable traditions is the offering of liquor to the deity. Devotees believe that offering alcohol, specifically country-made liquor, to Lord Bhairav pleases him and ensures protection and blessings. This practice is unique to this temple and attracts devotees seeking the deity's favor.

**Historical Significance:**

The Kal Bhairav Temple has a long history and is considered one of the ancient and important temples in Varanasi. It has been a site of worship and reverence for centuries, and its origin is attributed to the ancient times when the city was believed to be the abode of Lord Shiva. The Kal Bhairav Temple in Varanasi holds significant historical and cultural importance. Here are some key points regarding the historical significance of the temple:

**Ancient Origins:** The Kal Bhairav Temple has a long history that dates back several centuries. It is believed to have existed since ancient times, and its origin is associated with the rich mythology and legends of Varanasi. The city of Varanasi itself is considered one of the oldest inhabited cities in the world, and the temple is regarded as one of its ancient landmarks.

**Connection to Hindu Mythology:** The temple is dedicated to Lord Kal Bhairav, an incarnation of Lord Shiva in his fierce form. According to Hindu mythology, Lord Kal Bhairav is the protector and guardian deity of Varanasi. It is believed that he safeguards the city and its devotees from negative forces and evil influences.

**Spiritual Significance:** The Kal Bhairav Temple holds immense spiritual significance for devotees, particularly those seeking protection, courage, and blessings from Lord Bhairav. Devotees believe that offering prayers and performing rituals at the temple can ward off obstacles and bring about auspiciousness in their lives.

**Cultural Heritage:** The temple is an integral part of Varanasi's cultural heritage. It is deeply interwoven with the city's religious and cultural fabric and plays a vital role in the religious practices and traditions of the local community. The temple's rituals, festivities, and unique practices, such as the offering of liquor, contribute to its distinct cultural identity.

**Pilgrimage Destination:** The Kal Bhairav Temple attracts a large number of devotees and pilgrims throughout the year. Many people visit the temple as part of their spiritual journey or as a religious pilgrimage to Varanasi. The temple's historical significance and association with Lord Bhairav make it a revered destination for devotees seeking divine blessings.

The Kal Bhairav Temple stands as a testament to the enduring cultural and religious heritage of Varanasi. Its historical significance, deep-rooted mythology, and spiritual aura make it a significant place of worship and devotion. The temple's ancient origins and connection to Hindu mythology contribute to its historical importance and continue to draw devotees from far and wide.

### Architecture

The temple showcases traditional North Indian architectural style, characterized by its stone structures and carvings. The main shrine of Lord Kal Bhairav is located within the temple complex, and the deity is adorned with traditional clothing and ornaments. The temple complex may also include other smaller shrines dedicated to other deities. The architecture of the Kal Bhairav Temple in Varanasi reflects a traditional North Indian style with its characteristic elements.

**Here are the key architectural aspects of the temple:**

**Structure:** The Kal Bhairav Temple has a compact and simple structure, typically constructed with stone or brick. The temple is designed in a rectangular or square shape and follows a basic layout with a central sanctum housing the deity and a surrounding open courtyard.

**Temple Facade:** The temple facade is adorned with intricate stone carvings and sculptures. The carvings often depict mythological figures, deities, and intricate patterns. The exterior walls may feature decorative motifs such as lotus flowers, elephants, or other sacred symbols.

**Gopuram:** The temple usually has a prominent entrance gate, known as the gopuram. The gopuram is a towering structure adorned with elaborate carvings and sculptures. It serves as the main entrance to the temple complex and leads to the central courtyard.

**Sanctum Sanctorum:** The central sanctum, also known as the garbhagriha, houses the main deity, Lord Kal Bhairav. The sanctum is a small chamber with minimal decoration to maintain a sacred and reverential ambiance. The idol of Lord Kal Bhairav is usually made of stone and may be adorned with traditional clothing and ornaments.

**Courtyard and Open Space:** The temple complex often includes an open courtyard surrounded by pillared verandas or corridors. The courtyard serves as a space for devotees to gather and perform religious rituals. It may have smaller shrines dedicated to other deities and areas for offerings and prayer.

**Decorative Elements:** The temple architecture incorporates decorative elements such as ornate arches, sculpted pillars, and intricate ceiling designs. These elements showcase the skill and craftsmanship of the artisans and add to the aesthetic appeal of the temple.

The architecture of the Kal Bhairav Temple is simple yet visually striking. The focus is on creating a sacred and serene atmosphere for devotees to offer their prayers and seek the blessings of Lord Kal Bhairav. The temple's design and adornments reflect the rich artistic traditions of North India and add to the cultural and religious significance of the temple. The Kal Bhairav Temple holds immense spiritual significance for devotees who seek the blessings and protection of Lord Bhairav. The temple's unique rituals and practices, such as the offering of liquor, make it a distinctive and intriguing place of worship in Varanasi.

# Chapter 7.6: Annapurna Temple

The Annapurna Temple in Varanasi is a revered Hindu temple dedicated to Goddess Annapurna, the goddess of food and nourishment.

**Here is some information about the Annapurna Temple:**

**Location:** The Annapurna Temple is located in the Kashi Vishwanath Temple complex in Varanasi, Uttar Pradesh, India. It is situated near the famous Dashashwamedh Ghat, one of the prominent riverfront ghats in Varanasi.

**Deity:** The temple is dedicated to Goddess Annapurna, who is considered the provider of nourishment and sustenance. Annapurna is regarded as a form of the goddess Parvati, the consort of Lord Shiva. Devotees worship Goddess Annapurna to seek her blessings for abundance and fulfillment in their lives.

**Architecture:** The Annapurna Temple exhibits a North Indian architectural style with intricate stone carvings and sculptures. The temple structure is typically made of stone and features a sanctum sanctorum where the main deity, Goddess Annapurna, is enshrined. The temple facade often displays decorative elements such as ornate arches and engraved panels.

**Religious Significance:** The temple holds immense religious significance for devotees, particularly those seeking blessings for food, nourishment, and prosperity. It is believed that worshipping Goddess Annapurna with devotion can bring about fulfillment of material needs and spiritual nourishment.

**Annakoot Festival:** The Annakoot Festival, also known as Annakut or Govardhan Puja, is a significant annual festival celebrated at the Annapurna Temple. It falls on the day after Diwali, and it involves the offering of a variety of food items and delicacies to Goddess Annapurna. Devotees offer a large assortment of vegetarian dishes as a symbol of gratitude and seek her blessings for abundance and well-being.

**Feeding the Needy:** One of the notable aspects associated with the Annapurna Temple is the tradition of providing free meals to devotees and the needy. The temple administration often organizes community kitchens where meals are prepared and served to visitors, ensuring that no one goes hungry.

The Annapurna Temple in Varanasi is a place of devotion and reverence, where devotees seek the blessings of Goddess Annapurna for sustenance and abundance. The temple's architectural beauty, religious significance, and the noble practice of feeding the needy contribute to its importance as a spiritual and humanitarian center in Varanasi.

**Architecture And Religious Significance Of Annapurna Temple**

The Annapurna Temple in Varanasi exhibits a distinct architectural style and holds significant religious significance. Here's a closer look at its architecture and religious importance:

**Architecture:**

Structure: The Annapurna Temple follows the traditional North Indian architectural style. It typically features a compact structure made of stone or brick. The temple may have multiple levels and often includes a sanctum sanctorum where the main deity, Goddess Annapurna, is enshrined.

**Ornate Facade:** The temple facade is adorned with intricate carvings and sculptures, showcasing the artistic skills of the craftsmen. Decorative elements such as arches, pillars, and engraved panels can be seen on the exterior walls of the temple. The carvings may depict religious motifs, floral patterns, or scenes from Hindu mythology.

**Sanctum Sanctorum:** The central sanctum of the Annapurna Temple houses the idol or image of Goddess Annapurna. The sanctum is often decorated with flowers, garlands, and other traditional offerings. Devotees offer prayers and perform rituals in front of the sanctum to seek the blessings of the goddess.

**Religious Significance:**

**Goddess Annapurna:** The Annapurna Temple is dedicated to Goddess Annapurna, who is revered as the goddess of food and nourishment. Devotees worship her to seek blessings for abundance, prosperity, and fulfillment of their material needs. It is believed that Goddess Annapurna's blessings can provide sustenance and nourishment in both the physical and spiritual realms.

**Offering of Food:** The temple holds a special significance in the context of food offerings. Devotees offer various food items to Goddess Annapurna as a symbol of gratitude and seek her blessings for a bountiful harvest, well-being, and sustenance. The act of offering food is considered an act of selflessness and devotion.

**Annakoot Festival:** The Annakoot Festival, celebrated at the Annapurna Temple, is a significant annual event. It usually takes place on the day after Diwali and involves the offering of a large variety of food items to Goddess Annapurna. Devotees prepare and present a mountain-like arrangement of food, symbolizing gratitude for the abundance and blessings received.

**Feeding the Needy:** The Annapurna Temple is also known for its charitable activities. The temple administration often organizes free food distribution to devotees and the needy. This practice of feeding the hungry is considered an act of compassion and service to society.

The architecture of the Annapurna Temple showcases the rich cultural heritage of Varanasi, while its religious significance lies in the worship of Goddess Annapurna and the act of offering and sharing food. The temple serves as a spiritual sanctuary where devotees seek blessings for sustenance, prosperity, and the fulfilment of their material and spiritual needs.

**Historical Significance Of Annapurna Temple**

The Annapurna Temple in Varanasi holds historical significance due to its association with the ancient city of Varanasi and the reverence for the goddess Annapurna.

**Here are some points regarding its historical significance:**

**Ancient Origins:** The Annapurna Temple is believed to have ancient origins, rooted in the rich historical and cultural heritage of Varanasi. The city of Varanasi itself is considered one of the oldest continuously inhabited cities in the world, with a history that dates back thousands of years. The temple stands as a testament to the enduring religious traditions and practices of the region.

**Vedic Connections:** Varanasi, also known as Kashi, has been a prominent center for religious and spiritual practices since ancient times. It holds great significance in Vedic literature and scriptures. The Annapurna Temple, dedicated to the goddess of nourishment, aligns with the ancient Vedic traditions that emphasized the importance of food, sustenance, and offerings to deities.

**Cultural and Social Influence:** The Annapurna Temple has played a significant role in shaping the cultural and social fabric of Varanasi. The temple and its associated festivals, such as the Annakoot Festival, have become an integral part of the cultural calendar and community life. The act of offering and distributing food has created a sense of social cohesion and shared responsibility within the community.

**Patronage and Development:** Over the centuries, the temple has received patronage from various rulers, dynasties, and devotees. Their contributions have led to the expansion, renovation, and embellishment of the temple complex. The temple's historical significance is also reflected in the architectural styles and decorative elements added by different patrons over time.

**Continuity of Worship:** The Annapurna Temple has maintained a continuous tradition of worship and devotion to the goddess Annapurna. The temple has served as a focal point for devotees seeking blessings, offering prayers, and participating in religious rituals associated with the goddess. The continued reverence for Goddess Annapurna highlights the enduring historical significance of the temple.

The historical significance of the Annapurna Temple lies in its connection to the ancient city of Varanasi, its alignment with Vedic traditions, and its role in shaping the cultural and social fabric of the region. The temple's history, patronage, and continuity of worship contribute to its importance as a sacred place and a symbol of devotion to the goddess of nourishment.

# Chapter 7.7: New Vishwanath Temple

The new vishvanath temple is situated admist the premises of banaras hindu university it is a replica of the kashi vishvanath temple situated in Varanasi. Shri kashi vishvanath mandir was destroyed and subsequently reconstructed over and over by various then reigning Mughal emperors. Hence, Pandit Madan Mohan Malviya decided to replicate this temple and marked its foundation stone in 1916 in the lush green campus of the university. It is located right at the heart of the university, opposite the iconic Sayaji Rao Gaekwad Library, BHU

Business tycoon Jugal Kishore Birla and the birla family promised Malviya ji to undertake the responsibility of replicating this temple and laid down its foundation in 1931. A beautiful edifice erected in white marbles and surrounds by a large garden took 35 prolonged years to finally opem its gate for the visitirs in 1966. Vishwanath temple in Varanasi is one of the most magnificent temples built by birla family in different cities across india and is therefore also known by the name 'Birla Temple'.

Interior of the New Vishvanath Temple

Shikhara of the New Vishvanath Temple

With its Shikhara's height being around 250 feet, it has the tallest temple tower in the world. The walls of the temple are engraved with the verses of Bhagavad Geeta along with their meanings and other pictorial inscriptions. Despite beinga Shaivite temple, it has nine other temples within the same structure and it welcomes devotees of all faiths.

Wall of the New Vishvanath Temple

The forecourt of the temple is every bhu student's go-to-hub, be it biryhdays or random hangouts. The Shiva shrine is in the ground floor and the Lakshmi Narayan[1] and Durga[2] shrines are on the first floor. Other shrines within Shri Vishwanath Mandir are Nataraj[3], Parvati[4], Ganesha[5], Panchmukhi Mahadev[6], Hanuman[7], Saraswati[8] and Nandi[9]. Entire text of Bhagavad Gita[10] and extracts from sacred Hindu scriptures are

1. https://en.wikipedia.org/wiki/Lakshmi_Narayan

2. https://en.wikipedia.org/wiki/Durga

3. https://en.wikipedia.org/wiki/Nataraj

4. https://en.wikipedia.org/wiki/Parvati

5. https://en.wikipedia.org/wiki/Ganesha

6. https://en.wikipedia.org/wiki/Sadasiva

7. https://en.wikipedia.org/wiki/Hanuman

8. https://en.wikipedia.org/wiki/Saraswati

9. https://en.wikipedia.org/wiki/Nandi_(bull)

inscribed with illustrations on the inner marble walls of the temple

---

10. https://en.wikipedia.org/wiki/Bhagavad_Gita

# Chapter 7.8: Vishalakshi Temple

Vishalakshi Temple is a renowned Hindu temple located in Varanasi, Uttar Pradesh, India. It is situated on the banks of the holy River Ganges and is dedicated to Goddess Vishalakshi, a form of Goddess Parvati.

**Location:** The temple is situated near the famous Manikarnika Ghat in Varanasi. It is located in the narrow lanes of the old city, known as the Kashi Vishwanath Lane.

**History:** The exact origins of the temple are not well-documented. However, it is believed to have been built around the 18th century. The temple holds great significance for followers of the Shakta sect, who worship the feminine aspect of the divine.

**Architecture:** Vishalakshi Temple exhibits traditional Hindu architectural style. It has a tall shikhara (spire) adorned with intricate carvings and sculptures. The sanctum sanctorum houses the deity of Goddess Vishalakshi, depicted with multiple arms, seated on a lotus.

**Significance:** The temple holds immense religious importance for devotees, especially women seeking the blessings of Goddess Vishalakshi. It is believed that the goddess bestows her devotees with courage, strength, and protection. Many people visit the temple to offer prayers and seek blessings for the well-being of their families.

**Festivals:** Various Hindu festivals are celebrated with great fervor at Vishalakshi Temple. Navaratri, the nine-night festival dedicated to the worship of Goddess Durga, witnesses significant celebrations here. The temple is beautifully decorated, and devotional songs and cultural programs are organized during this time.

**Temple Complex:** Apart from the main shrine, Vishalakshi Temple has a spacious courtyard where devotees can sit and meditate. The complex also houses smaller shrines dedicated to other deities, such as Lord Ganesha and Lord Hanuman.

Visiting Vishalakshi Temple provides an opportunity to experience the rich spiritual and cultural heritage of Varanasi, one of the holiest cities in Hinduism. Devotees and tourists can immerse themselves in the divine ambiance, seek blessings, and witness the religious rituals performed at the temple.

**Architecture**

The architecture of Vishalakshi Temple in Varanasi reflects the traditional Hindu style prevalent in the region.

**Here are some key architectural features of the temple:**

**Shikhara (Spire):** The temple's main structure is crowned with a tall shikhara, which is a characteristic feature of many Hindu temples. The shikhara is a curvilinear tower-like structure that rises above the sanctum sanctorum (garbhagriha) where the main deity is housed. It is adorned with intricate carvings and sculptures depicting various deities, mythological scenes, and motifs.

**Sanctum Sanctorum:** The sanctum sanctorum of Vishalakshi Temple houses the idol of Goddess Vishalakshi. It is a small and intimate space where devotees offer their prayers. The inner walls of the sanctum may be decorated with paintings or relief sculptures depicting scenes from Hindu mythology.

**Mandapa:** The temple complex typically includes a mandapa, which is a pillared hall or pavilion used for various religious and cultural activities. The mandapa provides an open gathering space for devotees and visitors. It is often adorned with beautiful carvings on the pillars and ceilings.

**Carvings and Sculptures:** The temple's architecture is known for its intricate carvings and sculptures that depict deities, celestial beings, floral patterns, and mythological scenes. These carvings are found on the temple walls, pillars, doorways, and other architectural elements. The craftsmanship reflects the artistic skills of the local artisans.

**Stone Work:** Vishalakshi Temple, like many ancient temples in Varanasi, is predominantly constructed using stone. Stone blocks are intricately carved and assembled to form the temple's structural elements, giving it a solid and enduring quality.

**Temple Complex:** In addition to the main shrine, the temple complex may include smaller shrines dedicated to other deities. These shrines often exhibit similar architectural styles and designs. The overall layout of the temple complex follows a planned and symmetrical arrangement, providing a serene and harmonious atmosphere.

The architecture of Vishalakshi Temple combines aesthetics, symbolism, and religious significance. It represents the rich cultural heritage of Varanasi and provides an architectural glimpse into the traditional temple design prevalent in the region.

**History and religious significance of Vishalakshi temple**

The history of Vishalakshi Temple in Varanasi is not extensively documented, but it holds significant religious and cultural importance The exact origins and construction date of Vishalakshi Temple are not well-established. However, it is believed to have been built around the 18th century. The temple has witnessed renovations and additions over the years, reflecting the evolving architectural styles of different periods. Annapurna[1], the goddess of food and form of Shiva's consort Parvati[2], is given the epithet Vishalakshi, the "wide-eyed". Her most famous temple stands at Varanasi, where patron goddess she is considered. The *Skanda Purana*[3] narrates the tale of the

1. https://en.wikipedia.org/wiki/Annapoorna_devi

2. https://en.wikipedia.org/wiki/Parvati

3. *https://en.wikipedia.org/wiki/Skanda_Purana*

sage Vyasa[4] cursing Varanasi, as no one in the city offered him food. Finally, Vishalakshi appears in the form of a housewife and grants food to Vyasa. This role of Vishalakshi is similar to that of Annapurna, who offers food to her husband Shiva, whose hunger can be satiated by her food. Shiva gratified by Annapurna's food, establishes Varanasi and appoints her as its presiding goddess. The goddess Vishalakshi of the Varanasi temple may have been identified with Annapurna in early times, however over time became a distinct goddess, resulting in the goddess temples.[18][5]

Vishalakshi, the "wide-eyed" goddess is often associated two other goddesses: Kamakshi[6], the "love-eyed" goddess of Kanchipuram[7] and Minakshi[8], the "fish-eyed" of Madurai[9], prominently because of their similar names.[19][10] Together the three are regarded the most important Goddess temples by South Indians. While Vishalakshi dwells in North India[11], the other goddess temples are in Tamil Nadu[12], South India[13]. South Indians venerated Vishalakshi for ages and have strong

---

4. https://en.wikipedia.org/wiki/Vyasa

5. https://en.wikipedia.org/wiki/Vishalakshi_Temple#cite_note-Arundhati2001-18

6. https://en.wikipedia.org/wiki/Kamakshi

7. https://en.wikipedia.org/wiki/Kanchipuram

8. https://en.wikipedia.org/wiki/Minakshi

9. https://en.wikipedia.org/wiki/Madurai

10. https://en.wikipedia.org/wiki/Vishalakshi_Temple#cite_note-Subramanian2003-19

11. https://en.wikipedia.org/wiki/North_India

12. https://en.wikipedia.org/wiki/Tamil_Nadu

13. https://en.wikipedia.org/wiki/South_India

ties with the temple. South Indian Tamil people[14] also helped renovate the temple in 1971

**Religious Significance:**

**Goddess Vishalakshi:** The temple is dedicated to Goddess Vishalakshi, who is considered a form of Goddess Parvati. Vishalakshi means "one with wide or large eyes." Devotees believe that the goddess possesses powerful and compassionate qualities. She is revered as the bestower of courage, strength, and protection.

**Shakta Tradition:** The temple holds great importance for followers of the Shakta tradition, which worships the divine feminine aspect of the Supreme Being. The Shakta tradition places emphasis on the worship of Goddess Shakti as the primordial energy and source of creation. Vishalakshi Temple serves as a significant center for Shakta devotees to connect with the divine feminine energy.

**Varanasi's Spiritual Significance:** Varanasi, also known as Kashi, is one of the holiest cities in Hinduism. It is believed to be the abode of Lord Shiva and Goddess Parvati. Vishalakshi Temple, located in Varanasi, adds to the city's spiritual aura. Devotees visit the temple to seek blessings, offer prayers, and experience the sacred energy associated with the city.

**Goddess' Blessings:** Devotees, particularly women, visit the temple to seek the blessings of Goddess Vishalakshi. They pray for the well-being and prosperity of their families, as well as for the fulfilment of their desires and aspirations. The temple is believed to provide solace, strength, and divine intervention to its devotees.

---

14. https://en.wikipedia.org/wiki/Tamil_people

**Festivals and Rituals:** Vishalakshi Temple celebrates various Hindu festivals with great enthusiasm. Navaratri, a nine-night festival dedicated to the worship of Goddess Durga, witnesses significant celebrations at the temple. Devotees participate in devotional singing, cultural performances, and religious rituals during this time.

Vishalakshi Temple stands as a revered place of worship, attracting devotees from different parts of the country and beyond. Its historical and religious significance, combined with its architectural beauty, makes it an important spiritual destination in Varanasi.

# Chapter 7.9: Mritunjay Mahadeva Mandir

The Mritunjaya Temple holds great significance for devotees of Lord Shiva. It is believed that offering prayers and seeking blessings from Mritunjay Mahadev can protect devotees from untimely death and bestow them with good health and longevity. Various rituals and ceremonies are performed at the Mritunjaya Temple, including the daily Aarti (devotional ceremony) and Rudrabhishek (anointing the deity with sacred substances). The temple attracts a large number of devotees, especially on auspicious occasions like Mahashivaratri, when special festivities take place. he temple is regarded as a place of spiritual power and divine blessings. Devotees visit the Mritunjaya Temple to seek relief from physical ailments, to overcome fears related to death, and to find solace in Lord Shiva's presence.

Mrityunjay Mahadev Temple in Varanasi is the very famous and glorious temple. This temple is the holy place of worship and belongs to the Lord Mahadev (Known as Lord Shiva by pilgrims).

The history of this temple is all behind an ancient well and "The Shivling". The meaning of the word Mrityunjay Mahadev is "The God who triumphs over of death". It is considered as, the Shivling in this temple keep away all the devotees from their unnatural death. Lord Shiva is worshiped as Mrityunjay Mahadev by devotees in order to get triumph over his unnatural death. People from all over India come here and perform "Mrityunjay Path" to get rid of their problems. In the campus of the temple there is an ancient well (also known as koop). The water of this well has therapeutic effect on human beings. It is considered as it has mixture of several underground water streams and has miraculous effect for curing numerous diseases.

Another story behind the magical well is that, a famous person "Dhanvantari" (father of the Ayurveda) has poured all his medicine in that well, that's why the water of this well is sacred and has medicinal effect as well as able to cure various diseases. Architecture: The temple features a traditional Hindu architectural style with intricate carvings and designs. It has a main shrine dedicated to Lord Shiva, where devotees offer prayers and perform rituals. The temple complex also includes smaller shrines dedicated to other deities.

## Chapter 7.10: Amethi Temple

Overlooking the sacred Ganges River, the Amethi Temple blends seamlessly into the riverfront vista of Banaras, the celebrated north Indian Hindu pilgrimage city (Its curvilinear towers mark the building as a Hindu temple following a longstanding architectural tradition, a choice befitting the temple's location in a city eulogized as the primordial Hindu sacred center. Underneath the superstructure, however, elegant cusped arches with blooming flowers, bracket sculptures in opulent courtly dress, and Hindu deities framed by Neoclassical pediments reveal the temple's more recent origin in 1854.

Like most of the temples, fortress-like residences, and broad flights of stone steps, called ghats, on Banaras's riverfront, the Amethi Temple is the product of extensive building activities and architectural experiments that began in Banaras in the eighteenth century and continued into the mid-nineteenth century. During this period, Banaras acquired a new importance as a major commercial and banking hub in addition to its previous status as a prestigious educational and religious center. The decentralization of the Mughal Empire (1526-1858) in the eighteenth century gave rise to new interregional networks of trade and politics, comprising burgeoning regional authorities[1], merchant groups, and bankers. Having emerged from humble beginnings, these newly established powerholders were eager, through cultural patronage, to reinvent themselves as a nobility with an ancient genealogy. Targeting Banaras for its religious and economic

---

1. https://upload.wikimedia.org/wikipedia/commons/7/7f/

India_in_1795_Joppen_High_Def.jpg

value, varying levels of emergent patrons—from local landholders to more distant ruling families with transregional influence—performed pilgrimages to the city and maintained its temple and palace complexes.

Built by multiple patrons near and far rather than a singular local dynasty, Banaras's temples present a compelling case study for exploring the mobility of objects, patrons, and artisans, and the negotiations between local and transregional forms. Some patrons brought their distinctive regional styles and building methods, seen in the wood and brick "Nepali temple" (1842), sponsored by the Nepalese royal family and modeled after the Pashupatinath Temple in Kathmandu. Others preferred to employ the building style and materials more widely available in the Banaras area. For the temples of Ahilyabai Holkar (r. 1767-1795), the pious queen of the Maratha Holkar dynasty, agents were dispatched from her capital in central India to hire local artisans. Moreover, the sources for Banaras's temples were not limited to temple architecture. In the more spacious suburbs away from the densely packed riverfront, domed cubical temples attached to Persian *char baghs* (four-part gardens) evoke Mughal tomb garden complexes. As George Michell has noted, Banaras may well be considered as an architectural "depository" of eighteenth- and nineteenth-century India.

The dynamic cultural exchanges seen in the temples built during this period have, however, only recently begun to receive scholarly attention. The reason is rooted in the historiography of Indian architecture, which, at its colonial origins in the late nineteenth century, set forth a paradigm based on rigid sectarian divisions and a narrative of decline.

The use of architectural vocabularies of Islamic origin, such as cusped arches and bulbous domes, in temple architecture was largely dismissed as a deviation from much earlier, "pure" Hindu temple forms current before the establishment of Islamic dynasties in India in the twelfth century. Drawing on studies that resist seeing "Hindu" and "Muslim" as distinctive stylistic categories and instead emphasize the synthesis of local and transregional visual languages, I reconsider the Amethi Temple in terms of its engagement with forms drawn from various cultural contexts.

Some of these forms, such as Neoclassical pediments, circulated across broad geographic zones even beyond South Asia and position the temple as a participant in global networks of objects, artisans, and patrons. At the same time, I also emphasize the significance of the temple's architecture and decorative program at the local and regional levels in Banaras and the province of Awadh, to which Banaras belonged until it was ceded to the British East India Company in 1775. I highlight how preexisting local forms were transformed to produce new and multiple meanings, rather than being "influenced" or supplanted by a dominant universal culture. Translation, as a multidirectional process of mediation, transformation, and circulation that traverses cultural and geographical boundaries, provides a useful framework for analyzing such encounters.

Yet its building date also marks the beginning of disdain for such eclecticism, the result of attempts to classify Indian architecture under sectarian categories and define the proper form of the Hindu temple as ancient and unchanging. If we consider the eighteenth century as "a time of flexibility, mobility, and possibility" before the "rigid academic taxonomies of the nineteenth century," the Amethi Temple stands at the overlap of these two moments. The 1850s in particular occupy the margins of Indian architectural history. In the historiography of South Asia, the long eighteenth century tends to end in the 1830s, when British political and economic dominance was secured over most of the Indian subcontinent. Scholarship on nineteenth-century Indian architecture, however, has largely bypassed the 1840s and '50s and has focused on the late nineteenth century, when the British Raj was firmly established, and on secular buildings that extensively engage with British architectural forms or are the product of British initiative. The Amethi Temple therefore defies a clear eighteenth- and nineteenth-century divide in the periodization of Indian architecture and prompts a more nuanced understanding of the transition between the two empires.

**Revival and Innovation**

The Amethi Temple stands above Manikarnika Ghat, the city's main cremation ground and one of the most frequently visited spots on the riverfront. Dedicated to the Hindu goddess Balatripurasundari, the temple is popularly known as the Amethi Temple in reference to its patron, Raja Madho Singh of Amethi (r. 1842-1891). At the time of the temple's construction, Amethi was a township of Sultanpur district in the province of Awadh, about 177 km northwest of Banaras. The temple's history reveals the great care and expense spent by the patron on what may have been his first major building project. The building was first completed in 1842, the same year the raja ascended to the throne in Amethi. When it was accidentally burned to the ground shortly after its completion, the raja promptly rebuilt the temple in its current form at an exorbitant cost of a *lakh* (100,000) of rupees in 1854. Its cost and scale far exceeded those of other temples built by Madho Singh in Amethi.

The Amethi Temple's coveted location on Manikarnika Ghat would have satisfied the new Raja's ambitions for visible legitimacy. Madho Singh came from a family of landowners (*taluqdar*) who began to formally use the title "raja," or king, only at the end of the eighteenth century. The Amethi ruling family claimed descent from the well-established Hindu Rajput Kachhwaha dynasty, whose members were among the most prominent patrons in Banaras during the sixteenth and seventeenth centuries. By emulating the pilgrimage and building practices of the Rajput Kachhwahas on the same stretch of ghats, Madho Singh could associate himself with a prestigious ancestry in the eyes of regional rivals and superiors.

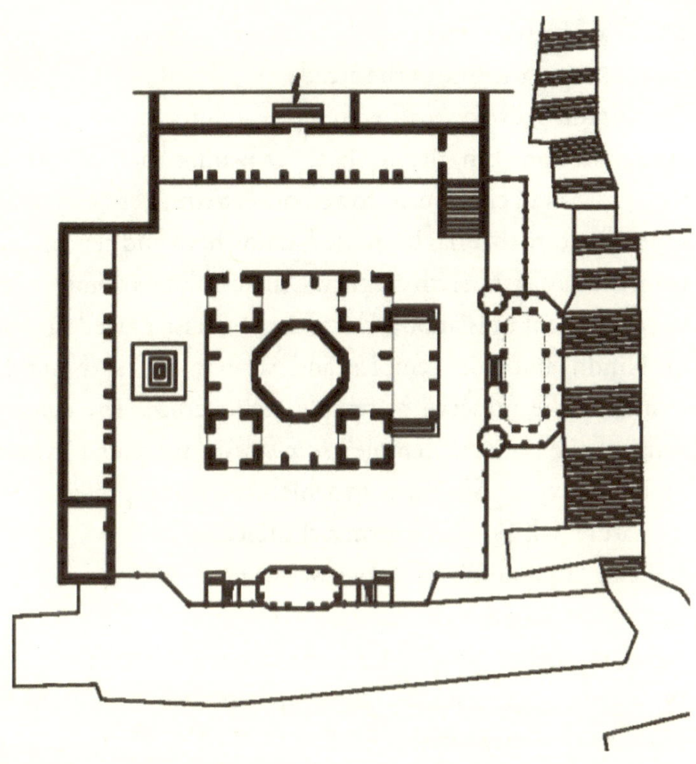

Detail from plan of the Amethi Temple on Manikarnika Ghat. Seen from the river, the Amethi Temple is a multi-storied structure divided into three levels: a basement level, a main level where the temple proper begins, and a superstructure. As it stands today, the main level is not accessible from the basement level. Instead, the main entrance to the temple is to the north in accordance with the temple's orientation, reached from the ghat by a steep flight of steps that are not visible from the river. As indicated above, the temple is built on a square five-shrine plan, with an octagonal sanctum and four smaller square shrines at the corners. Arcades with three cusped arches are placed between the four subsidiary corner shrines, whose walls have pierced screens (*jalis*) framed by blind cusped arches that continue the line of the arcade.

The building evokes earlier temple architecture in its most visible section. On the roofline, crowning each of the five shrines, is a tall curvilinear tower, or *shikhara*, a style of temple superstructure that has been used in northern and central India from as early as the sixth century. Unlike bulbous domes, which were prevalent in Islamic architecture, but also graced the roofs of Hindu and Jain temples and shrines, the *shikhara* had remained the preserve of temple architecture. The clustered form of the Amethi Temple's *shikhara*s in particular evokes a mode known as *Shekhari*, in which cascading projections of miniature half-*shikhara*s form a clustered tower.

Built in large numbers across western, central, and northern India between the eighth and tenth centuries, *Shekhari* temples regained their popularity from the eighteenth century onward In Banaras, for instance, all temple sanctums built by the Maratha Queen Ahilyabai Holkar (r. 1767-1795) featured the clustered *Shekhari* superstructure, including the Tarakeshvara Temple (1791), which stood directly under the Amethi Temple on Manikarnika Ghat. The choice seems to have been deliberately archaizing, as *Shekhari* temples had not been continuously built in the Awadh region, and domed and vaulted temples from the seventeenth century were more easily available as existing models.

. The Amethi Temple, Banaras

To characterize these temples simply as faithful replications of the medieval *Shekhari* mode would, however, be misleading. The architecture of the Amethi Temple defies a solely revivalist mode and is selective in its citation of past forms. In earlier *Shekhari* examples, the temple's ground plan, wall projections, and the cascading projections of miniature half-towers on the temple's superstructure correspond vertically with each other. At first glance, the superstructure of the Amethi Temple seems to follow this principle. The central *shikhara* above the sanctum stands atop a tall square drum divided into deep projections and horizontal moldings that evoke the walls of a medieval *Shekhari* temple.

The projections on the drum stand in exact correlation with the projections on the *shikhara* above. With the drum evoking what would be the walls of a medieval *Shekhari* temple, the superstructure creates the illusion that a complete temple stands on the roof. However, the projections of the drum and the *shikhara* bear no explicit connection to the flat walls of the sanctum at the main level, nor does the square plan of the superstructure reflect the octagonal form of the sanctum within the temple. Here, the *Shekhari* superstructure has been transformed from a fully integrated architectural modal system into a shallowly applied stylistic veneer.

Underneath the superstructure, the Amethi Temple stands still further apart from the *Shekhari* tradition. The building's concentric plan, in which the central sanctum is surrounded by arcades and corner shrines, seems to derive from more recent examples beyond Hindu temple architecture, such as palace buildings and Islamic tombs and shrines. The architectural historian Julia Hegewald, who has observed similar structures in Jain temples built after the sixteenth century, argues that the centrality of the main sanctum, achieved with concentrically arranged corridors, resembles the design principle of Islamic tombs.

Corner shrine doorway, Amethi Temple.

The cusped form of the Amethi Temple's arches recalls the façade of contemporaneous courtly architecture, as too does the use of *jali*s for the blind arcades of the corner shrines. With a history of power and wealth even newer than the Marathas', burgeoning regional authorities like Madho Singh were eager to adopt the visual trappings of elite courtly culture. Paradigms of this elite language abounded in Mughal and Rajput palaces. For example, the hall of private audience[2] in the Jaipur City Palace (c.1735), built by the Rajput Kachhwaha dynasty, features four corner chambers connected by arcades. In the corner shrine doorways of the Amethi Temple, a set of pilasters taking the form of Mughal baluster columns support the cusped arch

---

2. https://upload.wikimedia.org/wikipedia/commons/9/9e/
Jaipur-City_Palace-Diwan_I_Khas_VA-20131016.jpg

# Chapter 8: Sarnath

Sarnath is an ancient city located approximately 13 kilometres northeast of Varanasi (also known as Benares) in the state of Uttar Pradesh, India. It is one of the most important pilgrimage sites in Buddhism and holds immense historical, cultural, and religious significance.

Here are some key points about the historical significance of Sarnath:

1. Buddhist Heritage: Sarnath is one of the four main pilgrimage sites in Buddhism, known as the Four Holy Places. The other three are Lumbini (the birthplace of Buddha), Bodh Gaya (where Buddha attained enlightenment), and Kushinagar (where Buddha attained Parinirvana or final liberation).

2. First Sermon of Buddha: Sarnath is renowned as the place where Lord Buddha delivered his first sermon, known as the "Dhammacakkappavattana Sutta" (the "Turning of the Wheel of Dharma"). This event is considered the beginning of Buddha's teaching mission and the foundation of the Buddhist Sangha (community of monks).

3. Deer Park: The location where Buddha gave his first sermon is called the Deer Park because the Buddha's teaching was delivered to his five former companions who were ascetics and they, along with other animals, are believed to have been present at that time.

4. Symbol of Wheel of Dharma: In his first sermon, Buddha laid out the Four Noble Truths and the Eightfold Path, and this pivotal moment is

symbolized by the Dharmachakra or the Wheel of Dharma. This symbol is an essential representation of Buddhism and can be found all over Sarnath.

5.  Ashoka's Pillar: Emperor Ashoka, a significant patron of Buddhism, visited Sarnath around 3rd century BCE and erected a stupa here. His famous Ashoka Pillar still stands at the site. The pillar's capital features four back-to-back lions, which has now become the national emblem of India.

6.  Archaeological Significance: Sarnath is an important archaeological site with various stupas, monasteries, and other structures that provide valuable insights into ancient Buddhist art and architecture.

7.  Preservation of Buddhism: Despite facing decline over the centuries, Sarnath remained an important site for Buddhist pilgrimage and continued to be visited by pilgrims from various parts of the Buddhist world.

8.  Tourist Attraction: Today, Sarnath attracts tourists and pilgrims from all over the world who come to explore the rich Buddhist heritage, meditate, and pay their respects at the sacred sites.

Sarnath's historical significance lies not only in its association with the life of Buddha but also in its role as a beacon of Buddhist culture and spirituality throughout the ages. The preservation of this ancient site has allowed people to connect with the roots of Buddhism and learn from its teachings for generations.

## Dhamek Stupa

The most remarkable structure in Sarnath, India is *Dhamek Stupa*. It's a massive cylindrical structure measuring 28m in diameter and 43,6m in height. It marks the place where Buddha taught the Four Noble Truths and it's been enlarged on six occasions since its origin in 500 CE.

The front stone bears floral designs of the Gupta period and the wall of the stupa is covered with beautiful figures, geometric design and swastika signs. The word *Dhamek* is a distorted form of *Dharma Chakra* that means "turning the wheel of the Dharma". Buddha's first sermon was on the "Wheel of Law", which might be the reason for the name

**Buddhist Temple In Sarnath**

## Jain Temples

Varanasi is considered one of the holiest cities in Jainism, Hinduism, and Buddhism. While it is primarily known for its Hindu temples and ghats along the river Ganges, there are a few Jain temples in Varanasi as well. Here are some notable Jain temples in Varanasi:

## Shri Parshvanath Digambar Jain Temple (Sarnath):

Located in Sarnath, a suburb of Varanasi, this temple is dedicated to Lord Parshvanath, the 23rd Tirthankara of Jainism. It is a significant pilgrimage site for Jains, and the temple complex also includes a dharamshala (guesthouse) for devotees. Shri Parshvanath Digambar Jain Temple is a revered

Jain temple located in the holy city of Varanasi, specifically in Sarnath. Sarnath is a significant pilgrimage site for Jains as it is believed to be the place where Lord Parshvanath, the 23rd Tirthankara of Jainism, delivered his first sermon after attaining enlightenment.

The temple complex is dedicated to Lord Parshvanath and features an idol of the Tirthankara in a seated posture. The temple is known for its architectural beauty, intricate carvings, and serene ambiance, providing a peaceful environment for devotees and visitors.

Apart from the main temple, the complex also includes a dharamshala (guesthouse) that provides accommodation facilities for Jain pilgrims. Devotees visit this temple to seek blessings, offer prayers, and participate in various religious activities. The architecture of Shri Parshvanath Digambar Jain Temple in Varanasi is notable for its intricate craftsmanship and traditional Jain style. Here are some features commonly found in the architecture of Jain temples:

**Entrance and Gateways:** The temple usually has an elaborate entrance with a grand gateway called torana. The torana is adorned with ornate carvings, depicting Jain deities, celestial beings, and auspicious symbols. These gateways often have multiple levels and are intricately decorated.

**Shikharas (Spire):** The main temple structure is crowned with a shikhara, which is a spire-like structure. Jain shikharas are typically pyramidal and multi-tiered, featuring miniature shrines, sculptures, and detailed carvings. The shikhara is a prominent element of the temple and represents the spiritual ascent towards liberation.

**Mandapa (Pillared Hall):** Jain temples often have a mandapa, a pillared hall where devotees gather for prayers and religious ceremonies. The mandapa is usually supported by intricately carved pillars, showcasing motifs of Jain mythology, flora, and fauna. The ceilings of the mandapa are adorned with elaborate paintings or carvings depicting Jain legends.

**Garbhagriha (Sanctum Sanctorum):** The sanctum sanctorum of the temple, known as the garbhagriha, houses the main deity or idol. The garbhagriha is considered the holiest part of the temple and is designed to create a sacred atmosphere. The deity, in this case, the idol of Lord Parshvanath, is placed on a pedestal and is the focal point of worship.

**Sculptures and Carvings:** Jain temples are known for their exquisite stone carvings and sculptures. The walls, pillars, and arches of the temple are adorned with intricate artwork depicting Jain Tirthankaras, Yakshis (celestial beings), lotus motifs, and scenes from Jain mythology. The craftsmanship and attention to detail in these carvings are remarkable.

**Shri Suparshvanath Digambar Jain Temple (Sarnath):** Situated adjacent to the Shri Parshvanath Digambar Jain Temple in Sarnath, this temple is dedicated to Lord Suparshvanath, the 7th Tirthankara of Jainism. The temple features intricate architecture and beautiful idol of Lord Suparshvanath.

**Shri Sitalnath Jain Temple:** Located in Varanasi city, this temple is dedicated to Lord Sitalnath, the 10th Tirthankara of Jainism. The temple is known for its serene ambiance and intricate artwork.

**Shri Padmavati Digambar Jain Temple:** Situated near the Sitalnath Jain Temple in Varanasi, this temple is dedicated to Goddess Padmavati, the Yakshini (celestial attendant) of Lord Parshvanath. The temple is adorned with beautiful carvings and attracts devotees.

# Chapter 9: Sanskrit Sources For The Study Of Banaras

## 1. PURANAS

### Kashi Khanda

One of seven khandas, sections, of the Skanda Purana. The structure of the whole Skanda Purana. The structure of the whole Skanda Purana is based on the great tirthas of India. The Kashi Khanda is 100 chapters long and contains myths, mahatmyas, ritual prescriptions, and geographical information. In several chapters [ 83, 84, 97 ] the temples and tirthas of Kashi are located in relation to one another. The Kashi Khanda is not quoted by Lakshidhara [12th century], but certainly describes the ascendant Kashi of Gahadavala times. Since it cites old and new locations for several temples, its final compilation must have been after the destruction of majny of the city's temples in 1194. Sukul dates it in the mid-fourteenth century.

Kashi Rahasya, "The Secret Lore Of Kashi" Purported to be an appendix to the Brahmavaivarta

Purana, but not generally acknowledged as such. The work is both mystical in its identification of the city with Brahman, and ecumenical in its attempt to see the city as belonging to both Shiva and Vishnu. In general, it contains little geographical information, but it does contain the only major mahatmya of the Panchakroshi pilgrimage and its station. It contains twenty-six chapters and dates from the fourteenth to the seventeenth century.

## Kashi Kedara Mahatmya

The praise of the Kedara linga in Kashi. The work also purports to be a supplement to the scriptures, containing secrets held apart. It tells the story of how the Himalayan Kesara came to Kashi and praises the tirthas surrounding Kedara. It contains thirty-one chapters and dates from the fourteenth to the seventeenth century.

## Brahma Purana

Ancient mytho-historical accounts of the rivalry of the Kashis and Haihaiyas, containing the seed of the story of Divodasa. These accounts are from the earliest Puranic traditions, fourth to sixth centuries

## Matsya Purana

The 'Avimukta Mahatmya" its final verse mentions the famous five tirthas along the Ganges in Banaras.

It contains the myth of the yaksha who became Shiva's devotee, the story of Kapalamochana, and the story of Vyasa's bad temper in Kashi. It dates from the eighth to the eleventh century.

## Karma Purana

The "Varanasi Maharmya" told by Vyasa to Arjuna. It mentions the great lingas of ancient Kashi-Omkareshvara, Krittivaseshvara, Madhyameshvara, etc. The Kapalamochana story, beginning with the fiery linga and ending with Kala Bhairava's expiation of the sin of brahmin-killing, is told in II.32. it dates from the eighth to the eleventh century.

## Padma Purana

Diverse myths, mahatmyas, and diverse dates for its various sections.

## Vamana Purana

Brahmin-killing destroyed in Varanasi, eight to eleventh century.

## Linga Purana

'Varanasi Mahatmya" in praise of Avimukteshvara, eighth to eleventh century.

## Narada Purana

Praises various tirthas and lingas, especially Krittivaseshvara, Avimukteshvara, Omkareshvara. It dates from after the twelfth century, for the author plagiarizes from Lakshmidhara.

**Shiva Purana**

The creation of all, from Manikarnika. The mahatmya of Vishveshvara, twelfth to thirteenth century.

**Bhangavata Purana X.66; Vishnu Purana V.34.**

Account of Krishna's destruction of Kashi. A story with its seed in the most ancient Puranic traditions.

**Markandeya Purana**

The story of King Harishchandra.

**Agni Purana**

Short mention of the measurement of Varanasi and its several tirthas.

## Nibandhas

Tirthavivechana Kanda- "The discussion of Tirthas". One of the fourteen parts of Lakshmidhara's "Wishing tree of duties" the Krityakalpataru, it collects verses on the various tirthas, beginning with over 100 pages on Varanasi, then treating Prayaga, Gaya, Mathura, and others. The twelfth-century date provides a watershed for the dating of tirtha mahatmyas.

**Tirtha Chintamani-** "The wishing jewel of Tirthas". Part of the fifteenth-century digest called the Smriti Chintamani, compiled by Vachaspati Mishra, a scholar of Mithila, it deals with Gaya, Puri Prayag, Kashi and Ganga.

**Tristhalisetu-** "Bridge to the Three Sacred places". Compiled by Kashi's Narayana Bhatta in the sixteenth century, it consists of four sections; the 'General' section on pilgrimage, followed by section on Kashi, Prayaga, and Gaya.

**Tirtha Prakasha-** "The Glory of Tirthas". Indebted to the TS. Compiled by Mitra Mishra of Gwalior in the seventeenth century as part of the Viramitradaya.

# Conclusion

Banaras is not the story of bricks and stones, it is in fact a living history in itself. No other city of the world is like Varanasi, not even in India. Its place in Hindu mythology is virtually unrivalled. It has always been a great centre of learning, religion, art and culture, attracting people from all over the world- rich and poop, men and women, young and old, and even sick and dead. Hindus perceive Banaras as such a sacred place that if one leaves this world in Varanasi then his or her soul will undoubtedly go to heaven. Banaras is mosaic of Indian culture, representing all the diversity and distinctiveness of the regional cultures of India. People from all parts of India, speaking different languages and dialects and carrying their own culture inwardly, and becoming part of the mosaic culture of the city outwardly. It is a city where the past and the present mingle so beautifully that the joy of visiting it and even living in it is unforgettable. It has now become a large city with more than a million people, but the basic culture of the city has remained alive. Today Varanasi is a complex web of old and new, stability and change, industry and agriculture, and business and spirituality. To be in Varanasi is an extraordinary experience, an experience in self-discovery, an eternal oneness of the body and soul. It is a city where experience and discovery reach the ultimate bliss. Varanasi gives solace to millions of

Indians and a sense of wonder to thousands of foreigners each day and year. With the growth of global tourism and widespread interest in seeing culture in the mirror of history and tradition, religios heritage resource management becomes a critical issue in two primary ways

Protection and maintenance of sacred sites , and the survival and continuity of pilgrimage ceremonies that preserve centuries-old human interactions with the earth and its mystic powers.

Varanasi has been a sacred city of scholarship and wisdom. To continue and re-enforce the intellectual and spiritual tradition of the city universities like banaras hindu university, Sampurnanand Sanskrit University, Mahatama Gandhi Kashi Vidyapeeth and central university of Tibetan studies have been set up in relatively recent times. But the city appears to be losing its serenity and sacredness. Ganga, its soul, is polluted. The city has become so congested that it is difficult to reach the ghats and more difficult to have the darshan of Vishvanath. The past is there to inspire, the future is there in dreams; the present is the time to act. Some saints have given a lead. Let us hope that the caravan would lengthen and a time will come, sooner than later, to make Varanasi what it deserves to be.

Varanasi has an intangible heritage. It grew as an important industrial center, famous for its perfumes, carpets, brass and copper wear, glass bangles, ivory works, and a variety of handicrafts. The city is the best producer of silk drapes brocaded with metals like gold and silver thread called 'Banarasi Saree'. Varanasi has its won style of classical Indian music and has produces prominent philosophers, poets, musicians and writers in the Indian history.

CARPETS AND SAREES OF VARANASI.

HANDICRAFTS OF BRASS AND COPPER IN VARANASI

Varanasi runs purely on tourism, therefore festivals is another important attraction of te city. In November and December a five day music festival is organized by the Uttar-Pradesh

Tourism Department known as Ganga Mahotsava. On this occasion, the celebration of Ganga is attended by thousands of pilgrims who release lighted lamps to float in the river from the ghats.

GANGA MAHOTSAVA IN VARANASI

This heritage city is an outstanding example of an eternal human settlement, that represents a culture and human interaction with nature. the pressures of tourism growth and city expansion have had a definite toll on the rich heritage of the city. Both tangible and intangible heritage are degrading and falling to stand the vagaries of time. There is an immense need to control pollution and develop strategic and sustainable means of preserving the city ith one eye on the past and another in the future.

Page |

# Also by Swatantra Bahadur

Breaking Barriers: LGBTQ Rights and Social Justice
Blossom with confidence
"Depression: A Roller Coaster Ride"
Finding Your Voice
Rahul Gandhi: The Untold Story
100 Aspects on Nature
Love By An Introvert
Man Of Golden India "Narendra Modi"
India " Unity lies in Diversity"
Indian's Heritage of Kashi "Varanasi"